GENTLE PA

HAPPY KIDS

A Parent's Guide To Using Positive Discipline To Raise Children With High Self-Esteem

Samuel Pattinson

The Whole Brain Child

Guide to Raising a Curious Human Being and Revolutionary Strategies to Nurture Your Child's Developing Mind

Samuel Pattinson

Introduction

A Whole-Brain Child is a ground-breaking approach to the rearing of children with main criteria that supports active and flourishing development of the brain, which will ultimately lead to calmer, and happier babies. The "upstairs brain," which takes emotional decisions and balances, is under construction until the mid-20s. And, particularly in young children, the right brain and its emotions tend to rule over the left brain's reasoning. No wonder children quietly throw tantrums, fight, or sulk. By applying these results to day-to-day parenting, you can turn every outburst, disagreement, or anxiety into an opportunity to transform your child's brain and foster critical development.

Parents are often experts on the bodies of their children. They know Fever is a temperature over 98.6 degrees. They know how to clean a wound so that it won't become contaminated. They know the foods that will most likely leave their child wired before bedtime. But even the most loving, best-educated parents still lack basic brain knowledge. That is not surprising? Particularly when they consider the central role that the brain participates in every part of a child's life that parents care about: discipline, decision-making, self-awareness, school, relationships, etc. The brain actually decides pretty much who we are, and what we are doing. And learning how the brain changes in response to our parenting will help us grow a healthier, more resilient infant, as the brain itself is profoundly influenced by the interactions that we offer as parents. So, we want to bring you to the viewpoint of the whole mind.

We would like to clarify some basic brain concepts and help you apply your new knowledge in ways that encourage and make parenting more meaningful. They don't assume having a whole-brain child is going to get rid of all the problems that come with parenting. But by learning a few simple and easy-to-master concepts about how the brain works, you'll be able to understand your child better, react to stressful situations more effectively, and build a foundation for social, emotional, and mental wellbeing. What matters is how well you are parenting your child, and we'll provide you with simple, scientifically-based ideas that will help you establish a healthy relationship with your child that can help shape his brain well and give him the best chance for a safe, happy life.

The chapters in this book are projected to explain the development of brain in children in its early stages. How left part of the human brain is with its right part and how they are interlinked with the body. The human brain involves many revolutionary steps through which it passes, and finally, it reaches to developmental stage. During the developmental stage, the child's brain is observing every single act from his surroundings and is feeding those actions in his mind. If the child's brain is not nurtured in a right and way, he may adopt adverse effects from his surroundings, which may hurt the child throughout his whole life. This can make him a cynic and cynical person who will contribute negativity and destruction to society. The last chapter of this book is based on the importance of nurturing children's minds in a better and positive way so that he can contribute positivity and good deeds towards his society. It is essential to nurture a child's mind at a developmental stage in the right way.

Chapter 1: Early Development of Brain

The stage of starting years in a child's life is specifically crucial for health and growth later on. Some of the critical reasons for this is how rapidly the brain develops starting before birth and continuing into early childhood. As the brain continues to grow and evolve into adulthood, the first eight years will lay the groundwork for potential success in learning, health, and life. Since birth to age 5, the brain of a child grows more in life than at any other time. And early brain development has a profound impact on the ability of a child to learn and excel in both school and life. Babies need nutrition, security, and stimulation for healthy brain development in the earliest years of experience, especially from pregnancy to age three. Recent advances in neuroscience give new evidence of the event of a baby's brain during this time. As a result, we know that babies ' brains form new connections at a fantastic rate in their earliest years–according to the Developing Child Center at Harvard University, more than 1 million every second–a pace never again repeated. In the beginning years of life, the nature of a child's interactions-positive or negative-helps to form the development of their brain. The average baby's brain is about one-quarter of the average adult brain size when he is born. Incredibly, in the first year, this doubles in size. It continues to grow to about 80 percent of adult size by age 3 and 90 percent - almost fully grown -by age 5. The brain is the human body's command center. A newborn baby has all of the brain cells (neurons) they'll have for the rest of their lives, but it's the connections between those cells that make the brain work. Brain connections allow us to move about everything, think, interact, and do just about everything. To make these relations, the early years of childhood are crucial. Every second, at least one million new neural connections (synapses) are created more than at any other time in life. Different areas of the brain, like movement, language, and emotion, are responsible for different abilities and develop at different rates. Development of the mind builds on itself, as connections eventually connect in more complex ways. This allows the child to move, speak, and think in more complicated ways. The initial years are the most significant opportunity for the brain of a child to develop the connections that they need to be healthy, able, and successful adults. In these early years, the relationships required for many relevant, higher-level skills such as motivation, self-regulation, problem-solving, and communication are formed -or not formed. For those essential brain connections to be formed later in life, it is much more difficult.

The brain is a profoundly interrelated organ and works in a richly coordinated fashion with its many functions. Emotional well-being and social skills provide a strong foundation for developing cognitive abilities, and together they are the bricks and mortar that form the foundation of human evolution. All-important prerequisites for success in school and later in the workplace and community are the physical and emotional health, cognitive-linguistic capacities, and social skills that emerge in the early years. The brain's underlying architecture is built through an ongoing process that starts before the birth of a child, and it keeps going on into adulthood. Early childhood experiences significantly impact the quality of that architecture by establishing a solid or fragile foundation for all of the following learning, health, and behavior. More than 1 million new neural connections are created every second during the first few years of life. After this time of sudden increase and concentration, connections are decreased by a process called pruning, to make brain circuits more efficient. The first to develop sensory pathways such as those for essential vision and hearing, followed by early language skills and higher cognitive functions. In a prescribed order, connections proliferate and prune, with later, more complex brain circuits built on more rapid, more uncomplicated courses.

Genes form neural relationships and life experiences in the brain-building process – including proper nutrition, security, and stimulation from caregivers talking, playing, and sensitive attention. The mixture of nature and nurture will lay the foundation for the future of a child. Research in neuroscience has shown us early childhood is a time of tremendous brain development. The young brain changes shape and size in reaction to everything the first years experienced. New environment, life experiences, careers, and relationships can all influence how the minds of children get wired. Numerous advances in brain development studies have been made in the last decade. They now realize there is much more that takes place in the first five years to influence a child's development than previously thought. This is a critical time in guiding the healthy growth and development of a child's brain. This thing should be kept in mind that the development of the brain is not a linear, step-by-step process but a life-long cascade of waves.

1.1 Brain Development before Birth

Most of what scientists know about the development of the fetal brain comes from studying animal brains or examining human postmortem samples. This work has provided insight into the creation of brain structure, but it does provide little clues as to how functional structures are structured. The earliest human fetal brain function investigations date back to the 1950s. In labor, when researchers placed electrodes on the abdomen of a pregnant woman and the walls of her cervix, they could detect electrical impulses that signaled fetal brain activity. Researchers and scientists started to evaluate that specific patterns of electrical activity were associated with neurological abnormalities.9 Scientists began experimenting with fMRI in the 1990s to map the connections in various regions of the brain. The fMRI measures brain activity changes related to changes in blood flow. During fMRI, the patient typically performs a task – seeing, for example, images of faces or finger tapping –

while the machine scans his or her brain. Researchers are looking for brain areas that light up during the mission. By that point, neuroscientists knew there was much more functional happening than a stimulus or task could be tested, but it was unclear how these functions could examine in a better way. Then, in 1995, a fortuitous observation was made by then-graduate student Bharat Biswal: the brain produces signals all the time, even if it is not engaged in a task. The use of fMRI to quantify these resting-state signals allowed scientists to analyze brain activity for the first time, without the subject having to tap a finger as much as possible. Researchers turned to preterm infants in the search for answers about how and when brain networks are created. Nearly 10 percent of all babies around the world are preterm born, that is before the end of the 37th week of pregnancy. Those kids are more likely to develop autism spectrum disorders, attention-deficit / hyperactivity disorder, emotional disorders, and neurological abnormalities compared with term babies. Preterm infants are also more likely to experience cognitive difficulties and problems later in life. A growing body of research suggests that changes in the way the brain is wired before or shortly after birth can cause these cognitive impairments. These first experiments by Smyser and other researchers have shown that the communication channels of the brain were active, albeit in an embryonic state, before term birth. Preterm babies allowed researchers to study the production of neural processes typically found within the womb. Researchers have found it difficult to know, however, whether the patterns they saw in these infants represented the healthy development of brain communication networks.

Human brain formation begins shortly after birth and carries on into early adulthood. During the third week of gestation (pregnancy), the fetal brain starts developing. Neural progenitor cells begin to divide and differentiate into neurons and glia, the two types of cells which form the nervous system's base. Before we get into fetal brain development science, here's a short anatomy lesson on the brain of your infant. We're familiar with five different regions, each responsible for different functions:

Cerebrum: This is the central part of the brain, and it's responsible for thought, remembering, and emotions. This is where the cerebral cortex lives, with its distinct lobes (including the frontal and temporal lobes).

Cerebellum: Area responsible for engine control.

Brain stem: This is the engine that powers most of the vital functions of your baby, including heart rate, breathing, and blood pressure.

Pituitary gland: This pea-sized gland releases hormones that are responsible for growth, metabolism, and more in your body.

Hypothalamus: This area covers the temperature of the body, hunger, thirst, sleep, and emotions.

First Trimester

The neural layer of the female's fetus (think of it as the base of her baby's brain and spinal cord) develops just 16 days after conception. This grows longer and folds on itself until the fold becomes a groove, and that groove becomes a tube — the neural tunnel. Once the neural tube is closed, it bends and bulges into three parts at around week six or week 7 of pregnancy, commonly known as the forebrain, midbrain, and hindbrain. Just to the back of the hindbrain sits the section which will soon become the spinal cord of your infant. Finally, these areas spill into those five different brain regions with which we are most familiar: the cerebrum, the cerebellum, the brain stem, the pituitary gland, and the hypothalamus. All of these fetal brain regions, of course, require more time to be fully up and running.

At the same time, different neural cells develop and travel to form the very beginnings of nerves throughout the embryo. The nervous system of an unborn baby is comprised of millions upon millions of neurons; each of these small cells has itty-bitty branches branching off of them so that they can link and interact with each other. Baby's first synapses come with this, which essentially means that the baby's neurons can create and communicate initial movements in fetal like twisting and moving into the fetal position. Certain motions begin quickly, with a mother's fetus wiggling at around eight weeks to his developing limbs. By the ninth week, a thin, smooth structure emerges in the brain. The structure of the brain will change throughout pregnancy as it develops and begins to shape the characteristic folds which designate distinct brain regions. Changes in brain anatomy are indicative of significant cellular level changes. Neurons start producing the chemical signaling molecules in the different brain regions, which will allow contact between nerve cells. The fiber networks are emerging that will become the superhighway of information for the brain. The cells that make up the neocortex — the part of the brain that co-ordinates sight, sound, spatial reasoning, critical thought, and language — begin communications.

Second Trimester

Baby's brain directs steady contractions of the diaphragm and chest muscles during the second trimester (think of them as breathing movements). In about 16 weeks, Baby's first kick of sucking and swallowing impulses. By 21 weeks, the natural reflexes of the baby will allow him to take a few ounces of amniotic fluid every day. And all that swallowing also involves the taste of the infant, another concept that is in full gear now. The first kick of the baby can be felt by his mother in about 18 weeks of pregnancy (but don't panic if it takes a couple of weeks longer — that's normal, particularly among first-time moms). At about the same time, myelin covers the baby's nerves, protective insulation that speeds up communications between nerve cells (myelin keeps growing until the first birthday of your baby). And a further primary reflex happens at 24 weeks: Blinking. Little one's brainstem (controlling heart rate, breathing, and blood pressure) is almost fully mature at the tail-end of trimester two, sitting just above the spinal cord but below the cerebral cortex (the last region to mature). The fetal nervous system is being sufficiently developed to startle your baby from loud noises outside the womb— and may even turn his head towards the sound of your voice! Another promising development: Fetal brainwave activity includes sleep cycles at 28 weeks, including REM (the period when dreaming takes place).

Third Trimester

The third trimester is brimming with rapid neuronal growth and cabling. Baby's brain has approximately increased in weight over the last 13 weeks of gestation, rising from around 3.5 ounces at the end of the second quarter to about 10.6 ounces at the peak. And it also starts to look different: its once smooth surface becomes more grooved and indented. At the same moment, the cerebellum (motor control) is growing speedily— faster now than any other region of the fetal brain (it's surface area in the last 16 weeks of pregnancy increases30-fold). All of this development is excellent news for the cerebral cortex (think, recall, feel). Although this critical area of the brain multiplies during pregnancy, it only really begins to exercise nearly to the time when a full-term baby is born— and it matures slowly and progressively in the initial years of life, thanks to the enriching environment of the infant.

1.2 Stages of Brain Development

It continues to change all through the lifetime of the human brain. We cannot emphasize the importance of each point, and how we need to maintain and protect our growth rate of the mind from 0 to 100 and hopefully beyond. Let's look at every one of the five stages of human brain growth:

Step 1: 0 Months to 10 Months

Neurons and connections are increasing at a developmental stage in the mother's womb. A pregnant woman should have a healthy intake, including supplements like folic acid, B6 & B12, and should stay away from stress as much as possible, stimulate with sounds and sensations this young brain develops. Mum should avoid toxins, cigarettes, heavy metals, alcohol, and drugs. The body had been occupied with brain development until the child takes his first breath, preparing for life outside of the womb. Newborns have around 100bn neurons. It means that the average rate of brain cell development during pregnancy is about 250,000 new brain cells per minute. A child's brain at birth is about 60 percent of the size it will be when it is fully grown. The child's brain starts at about 20 cubic inches; then, in the first 90 days, after birth grows another 14 cubic inches, it comes close to doubling within the first three months. At conception, near the spinal cord is the only myelin-a fatty material that insulates the axons of your brain to help signals move faster. The brain area is responsible for core functions such as breathing, eating, and regulating heart rate.

Stage 2: Two Years to Six Years

Voluntary movement development, thought, cognition, frontal lobes involved in emotional development, associations, planning, working memory, and awareness. A sense of self develops, and experiences in life shape the psychological well-being. By the time the child is three years old, in terms of volume and brain cells, his brain is about 80 percent of his adult size. A three-year-old's mind is exceptionally sophisticated and maybe more [advanced] than any other animal on earth. At that point, as an adult, the brain has 200 percent more synapses. As the growth of the brain progresses, the mind of children tends to "prune" by breaking down specific synapses. Getting rid of the connections, it is not using helps the brain to concentrate its resources on the links that matter. The years leading up to the fifth birthday of a child are a part of the developmental "critical period." At this stage, experience forms the way synapses are shaped directly. Everybody's brain is adapted to their environment.

On the one hand, this means negative experiences will leave the child forever with a psychological scar. On the opposite side, it also means early intervention services, and more successful than ever attempt to reverse the effects of traumatic experiences. At age six, the brain is its adult weight and energy consumption peak at 95 percent. The caregivers must provide a nurturing environment and individualized contact daily. Harmful or harsh treatment may have future emotional consequences.

Stage 3: Seven Years to Twenty-Two Years

In terms of weight, teen brains appear adult-like, but they are not yet fully developed. Your body grew myelin from the back of the mind (which is responsible for the most basic functions) to the forehead (which has more complex circuits). The last area to be fully myelinated in the front lobe, which is essential for decision making, control of impulses, and empathy. The neural connections or' gray' matter are still pruning; brain wiring is continuing, the fatty tissues surrounding neurons or' white' matter are growing and helping to speed up electrical impulses and maintain connections. The prefrontal cortex is developed at the end, which involves regulating desires and making decisions. While the frontal lobe of an adult knows when to say "no" to peer pressure and threats, the ability has not yet been developed for teenagers. Parents should practice patience and provide guidance: To avoid poor choices, teens need "frontal lobe help." Adolescents, therefore, need to learn how to control careless, erratic, and irritable behavior. Do not use narcotics, caffeine, smoking, unprotected sex, and misuse of substances.

Stage 4: Twenty-Three Years Sixty-Five Years

Eventually, at age 22, the brain hits its peak power and lasts five more years. It is a downhill pattern afterward. Last to develop and first to go are the executive control brain circuitry that exists in both prefrontal and temporal cortices. Capacity to remember episodes is starting to decrease, processing speed slows, and less information is being processed in working memory.

Remaining mentally active, learning new things, staying physically active, and eating a very healthy diet is the best approach. Avoid drugs that change chemicals, cigarettes, alcohol, and mind. By the time you are in your mid to late 20s, your frontal lobe's brain development finally ended myelination — especially in the frontal lobes you need to assess. You will continue to shape and remove your entire life's synapses and brain cells. Still, there is one possible downside to your frontal lobe's development: mental illnesses such as schizophrenia or anxiety may now flare-up. Around 18 and 25 people are diagnosed with about 60 to 80 percent of people with major affective disorders. To be able to manifest these diseases, the frontal lobe needs to be connected to a point.

The brain slows down the production of brain cells and synapses in your 20s — plus it doesn't do as much "pruning" as it does — which is why you have a difficult time learning by the time you reach your 30s. Meanwhile, in the coming decades, your diet and exercise habits will set you up for a healthy-or forgetful-mind. Most people in their 50s begin to notice their mind slipping, starting with short-term memory. We're calling those' senior moments' and writing it off and making jokes. Nevertheless, only 5 percent of Alzheimer's diagnoses start early, so don't overlook signs that might be a sign of severe memory loss. One in ten adults age 65 and up is who Alzheimer's has. The risk doubles every five years after age 65, between the effects of biology and lifestyle. The causes of the condition aren't visible, but scientists do know that our brain cells and synapses are declining as we age. "These links go off, so the signals don't get from here to there. You look at an object, and you can suddenly no longer name it because you can't connect to the part of the brain where the name was stored.

Stage 5: Above Sixty-Five Years

Brain cells are damaged in critical areas such as the hippocampus, which is responsible for memory retrieval. Learn new skills, practice counseling to promote constructive feelings, exercise to improve abstract reasoning and concentration. Evite stress or include tension that decreases relaxation and exercises. Eat a healthy diet with foods to fuel one's dopamine level. By the time you reach 85, Alzheimer's risk is about 50 percent. This does not mean, however, that your memory's fate is sealed. While genetics play a part, brain-boosting behaviors and socializing can help test the mind. One method stands above the rest: "Aerobic exercise is by far the most potent thing. In a ten-year study involving more than 3,700 adults aged 60 and over, those who physically exerted the most had the giant brains and the lowest risk of dementia relative to those with the least physical activity. For those 75 and older, the protective effect was highest. Try every single day for 20 minutes of aerobics.

Chapter 2: Integration in Brain

Integration is the process whereby information from many sources is combined. The nervous system incorporates data from different senses (vision, hearing contact, etc.), and from many other parts of the brain, each part of the brain integrates information. This process is essential for the smooth and efficient functioning of the body and its components. It's also vital to the brain's ability to collect and organize world knowledge. The nervous system can achieve this because the neurons (nerve cells) have a portion (called dendrites) designed to incorporate or integrate information. We get contacts from many other neurons we call (synapses), and they integrate the signals from them. The core CNS nervous system is responsible for processing and reacting sensory information appropriately. It consists of two main components: the spinal cord acts as a communication medium between the brain and the rest of the body. It also controls necessary musculoskeletal reflexes without brain input.

The brain is both consciously and unconsciously responsible for integrating the most sensory information and for coordinating body function. Different parts of the brain function complex tasks such as thinking and feeling as well as control of homeostasis.

The human brain has more links than the stars in the universe. As an integrated system, this topic focuses on the brain and looks at how its many linked networks achieve synchronized results, connecting the mind to the brain and body.

2.1 Where Integration Occurs in Brain?

There are three main functions in the nervous system: sensory input, data integration, and motor output. Sensory input is when the body, via neurons, glia, and synapses, gathers information or data. The nervous system contains excitable nerve cells (neurons) and synapses that develop between the neurons and connect them throughout the body or with other neurons to centers. These neurons act on excitation or inhibition, and although nerve cells can vary in size and position, their function is determined by their contact with each other. Such nerves transmit impulses into the brain and spinal cord from sensory receptors. The data is then interpreted utilizing data processing, which only happens in the brain. After the brain has processed the information, signals are then transmitted from the brain and spinal cord to the muscles and glands, which are called motor production. Glia cells are present in tissues, and they are not excitable but aid with myelination, ionic regulation, and extracellular fluid. The nervous system consists of two major parts, the central nervous system (CNS) and the peripheral nervous system (PNS) or subdivisions. The CNS comprises the spinal cord and the spine. The brain is the "control center" of the body. Inside it, the CNS has different centers that perform the sensory, motor, and data integration. Such centers are subdivided into lower centers (including the spinal cord and brain stem) and higher centers by effectors that interact with the brain. The PNS is an extensive system of spinal and cranial nerves linked to the brain and backbone. It includes sensory receptors that aid in the perception of internal and external environmental changes. This information is transmitted to CNS by afferent sensory nerves. Then the PNS is subdivided into the independent nervous system and the somatic nerve network. The autonomic system involuntarily regulates internal organs, blood vessels, smooth and heart muscles. The bodily has voluntary skin, bones, joints, and skeletal muscle control. The two systems work together, joining and becoming part of the CNS by way of nerves from the PNS, and vice versa.

Functional Divisions of Nervous System

Scientists have been studying for decades how the sensory organs make the nervous system aware of the signals carried into the brain. These basic facts are well known: neural receptor cells translate external events— for example, light waves, skin sensations, or waves of air pressure— into electrical signals reaching the brain. Yet neuronal activity in the cerebral cortex does not contribute to conscious experience until it can be more elaborated. Ongoing sources of sensory information are converted into more complex combinations of features in higher-order areas from representations of essential components, in cardinal sensory cortical regions. Sensory stimuli are significant as a contrast to the latest and far away memories as well as perceptions. While numerous studies support the scheme described above, the physiological mechanisms remain unresolved. Depending on its functions, the nervous system can also be separated, but there are separate anatomical divisions and functional divisions. Both the CNS and the PNS contribute to the same roles, but these tasks can be traced to different brain regions (such as the cerebral cortex or hypothalamus) or peripheral ganglia. The problem with trying to fit functional variations into anatomical divisions is that several functions can sometimes be part of the same structure. The optic nerve brings signals from the retina that are used for the conscious perception of visual stimuli occurring in the cerebral cortex, or for the spontaneous reaction of even muscle tissue that is processed through the hypothalamus.

There are two ways of looking at how biologically the nervous system is split. Firstly, feeling, integration, and reaction are the essential functions of the nervous system. Secondly, body control can be somatic or autonomic — divisions primarily defined by the structures involved in the response. There is also an area of the peripheral nervous system called the enteric nervous system, which is responsible for a specific set of gastrointestinal-related functions within the domain of autonomic regulation.

The nervous system is to indulge in taking information about the world around us (sensation) and producing responses (motor responses) to that information. The nervous system is split into sections where sensation (sensory functions) and response (motor functions) are responsible. But there is a third feature to integrate. It is necessary to integrate sensory input with other sensations, as well as memories, emotional state, or learning (cognition). Many nervous system regions are called areas of convergence or association. The integration process integrates sensory perceptions and higher cognitive functions to create a response, such as memories, learning, and emotion.

2.2 Functional Imaging of Mind

Functional imaging is the examination of human brain function focused on the analysis of data obtained using brain vision modalities such as electroencephalography (EEG), magnetic encephalography (MEG), functional magnetic resonance imaging (fMRI), positron emission tomography (PET) or optical imaging. In terms of biology, technical architecture, and dynamics, the goal is to understand how the brain works. The framework for conducting these studies includes classical neuroanatomy, neurophysiology, and experimental psychology and cognitive neurosciences techniques, as well as more theoretical approaches based on computational neuroscience and statistics perspectives.

Modern functional visualization has two significant advantages over the multi / single-unit recordings used to study neuronal electrophysiology. It is generally non-disruptive and is thus regularly acceptable in humans. This enables the study of uniquely human attributes, like language. The second is that it can deliver a broad field of view. Instead of recording information about a single or small number of neuronal cells, an image may be collected, which summarizes simultaneous activity across the entire brain. This provides a different yet complementary view of neural coding (see, for example, functional integration, below). Nonetheless, a drawback is that functional imaging provides neuroscientists with only an approximate indicator of the quantities of primary interest, e.g., firing rates and membrane potentials.

Functional Analysis

The study of usable image data includes two key themes. We represent the ongoing debate about functional specialization versus functional integration within the brain in neuroscience.

Functional Specialization

The first is brain ' mapping' where three-dimensional neuronal stimulation images are generated, showing which parts of the brain are responding to a specific cognitive or sensory challenge. This is also term as the examination of functional specialization and usually takes some form of Statistical Parametric Mapping (SPM) to proceed. A classic example is the recognition of the human V4 and V5, the specialized areas for color and motion processing.

SPM is a voxel-based approach to reflecting on regionally specific responses to experimental stimuli, using classical statistics and topological inferences. PET or fMRI data are first processed spatially to conform to a specified anatomical space where responses are usually classified statistically using the General Linear Model (GLM). The GLM embodies a hemodynamic response convolution model for fMRI results. This accounts for the fact that neuronal response is a delayed and dispersed version of BOLD signals. At each voxel, GLMs are fitted, and inferences are made, in a statistical sense, about which parts of the brain are active. SPM techniques use Random Field Theory (RFT) and other analytical methods, e.g., False Discovery Frequency, to accommodate the spatial complexity of the image data (and compensate for numerous statistical comparisons made). The SPM technique can also be used to identify brain regions that have a higher gray matter density Using structural evidence. This is known as Voxel-Based Morphometry (VBM) and was used to demonstrate, for example, that the posterior hippocampus, which is useful for spatial navigation, is being expanded in taxi drivers. Data can be analyzed in sensor space for MEG or EEG to furnish a crude spatial mapping of brain function.

Nevertheless, functions may be more precisely defined using methods of source reconstruction. They function by using Maxwell's equations, setting a forward model explaining how a current source in the brain propagates to become a MEG or EEG measurement. Then invert these equations using statistical inference. The averaging technique is often used to analyze data from sensory systems. To order to produce an Event-Related Potential (ERP), the data immediately following a sensory event, e.g., hearing an audible sound, is averaged over several occasions. ERP modules can then be distributed into different parts of the brain. However, other cognitive components aren't easily isolated from this ERP approach. A characterization of time-frequency may be more appropriate for these.

Functional Integration

Functional integration is the knowledge of knowing the working of brain regions work together to process the responses to information and effect. Although functional integration often relies on anatomical knowledge of the connections between brain areas, the emphasis is placed on how large clusters of neurons–numbering in the thousands or millions–fire together under different stimuli. The broad datasets required for such a detailed brain function image have inspired the development of several novels and general methods for statistical interdependence analysis, such as dynamic causal modeling and statistical linear parametric mapping. Such samples are usually obtained by non-invasive approaches such as EEG / MEG, fMRI, or PET on human subjects. The findings can be clinically useful by helping to define the regions responsible for psychiatric disorders, as well as determining how different activities or habits affect brain function. There is a distinction drawn in functional integration between functional connectivity and effective connectivity. It is stated that two brain regions are functionally connected when there is a high correlation between the times the two are firing, although this does not imply causality. In comparison, efficient connectivity is a summary of the causal relationship between various regions of the brain. While statistical evaluation of the functional connectivity of multiple brain regions is non-trivial, determining the causality of which brain regions have a much thornier influence on which to fire, and requiring solutions to imposed optimization problems.

Several previous fMRI studies found that spontaneous activation of functionally related brain regions occurs during the resting state, even when there is no stimulus or movement of any kind. Human subjects faced with a visual learning task experience functional connectivity changes in the resting state for up to 24 hours, and complex practical connectivity experiments have even demonstrated alteration in professional association during a single scan. Taking fMRI scans of subjects before and after learning exercise, as well as the next day, it was shown that the practice caused a change in the hippocampal activity in the resting-state. Dynamic causal modeling revealed that, although there was no learning-related improvement in any visual field, the hippocampus also demonstrated a new level of successful communication with the striatum. The mixture of fMRI with DCM on subjects achieving an understandable task allows one to delineate which brain systems are involved in different learning sorts, whether implicit or explicit and documenting these tasks for a long time leads to changes in brain activation of the resting-state.

2.3 Brain and Body Integration

For many, it is easier to focus on physical health because it yields tangible results. You can look at the scale, look in the mirror, or search on your move counter for your mile log. Mental & emotional wellbeing is challenging to see outwardly, which is one reason why these areas can be daunting for change. New technologies hit the marketplace faster than we can keep up. New brain areas are being discovered, and new ways of imaging the brain are becoming a reality. The notion of an intricate laboratory or medical system to track brain activity is obsolete, and technology is now available to better integrate mind & body. The question of mind and body concerns to what degree the mind and the body are different or the same thing. The intention is about mental processes, perceptions, and knowledge. The body is concerned with the brain-neuron physical aspects, and how the brain is organized. Is the subconscious part of the mind, or part of the consciousness of the body? If they're different, how do they communicate then? And which of the two is responsible for this? Several theories were put forward to understand the relationship between what we call your mind (defined as the' you' conscious thinking that experiences your thoughts) and your brain (that is, part of your body). The connection between our minds and our bodies is something we feel instinctively, but how much attention do we pay each moment to your bodily sensations? We need a more profound awareness to understand our own emotional lives and those of the people around us, achieved through the practice of mindfulness and the development of body intelligence. Human beings are artifacts of material form. We have weight, solidity, and a variety of solids, liquids, and gases. Unlike other material objects (e.g., rocks), however, humans also can make decisions and justification for their existence. We've got' minds' in short. Usually, humans are described as possessing both a (nonphysical) account and a physical body/brain. This is called dualism. Dualism is the concept that the body and mind are both separate entities. Descartes / Cartesian dualism claims that mental and physical stimuli interact in two forms. Descartes has argued that the brain at the pineal gland interacts with the body. This form of dualism or duality implies that the mind influences the body, but the body can also have an impact on the rational mind, for instance, when people act out of emotion. Most of the previous accounts had been uni-directional about the relationship between mind and body.

Research Study on Mind-Body Connection

It has been shown in the studies for the first time that practicing meditation in mindfulness or being involved in a support group has a significant physical impact on breast cancer survivors at the cellular level. A group working from the Tom Baker Cancer Center of Alberta Health Services and the Department of Oncology at the University of Calgary has shown that telomeres— protein complexes at the end of chromosomes — retain their duration in survivors of breast cancer who practice meditation or are active in support groups while shortening without intervention in a comparison group. While telomeres ' disease-regulating properties are not fully understood, shortened telomeres are associated with multiple disease states as well as cell aging. In contrast, longer telomeres are thought to be disease-protective. "We also know that psychosocial techniques such as mindfulness meditation can help you feel better emotionally, but now we have evidence for the first time that they can also affect key aspects of your physiology," says Dr. Linda E. Carlson, Ph.D., Principal Investigator and Research Director at the Tom Baker Cancer Centre's Psychosocial Services Division. "It was interesting that over the three months examined, we could see any difference in telomere length," says Dr. Carlson, who is also a U of C professor at the Cumming School of Medicine and Faculty of Arts, a member of the Southern Alberta Cancer Institute. "To further measure these potential health benefits, more research is needed, but this is an exciting finding that provides encouraging news."

For the duration of the research, a total of 88 survivors of breast cancer who had finished their medical care for at least three months were involved. The average age was 55, with most patients completing treatment two years ago. We also had to experience significant levels of emotional distress to be successful. Participants attended eight weekly, 90-minute group sessions in the Mindfulness-Based Cancer Recovery group that offered guidance on awareness reconciliation and gentle Hatha yoga, intending to promote present-day un judgmental knowledge. Participants were also asked to perform 45 minutes of meditation and yoga per day at home.

Members met for ninety minutes weekly for twelve weeks in the Supportive Expressive Therapy group and were encouraged to talk freely about their problems and feelings. The aims were to develop mutual support and direct women in sharing, rather than suppressing or repressing, a wide range of both challenging and constructive emotions. Placed randomly in the control group, the participants attended one, six-hour seminar on stress management. Both participants in the study had blood tested and the duration of telomeres assessed before and after the involvement. Scientists have shown a short-term impact of these interventions on the length of the telomere as compared to a control group, but it is not known whether the effects last. Dr. Carlson says another path for further studies is to see if psychosocial approaches have a positive impact beyond the study period of three months. Allison McPherson was first diagnosed in 2008 as having breast cancer. She was put within the mindfulness-based cancer recovery group when she joined the study. She says today that experience has changed one's life. "At first, she was cynical and thought it was a lot of hocus-pocus," says McPherson, who underwent a whole year of chemotherapy and many surgeries. "But she was now practicing conscientiousness throughout the day, and it encouraged her to become less aggressive, childlike towards her and others." Research participant Deanne David has also been put in the focus group. "It made a great contrast to her to be part of this," she says. "People on their cancer journey will benefit from learning more about the knowledge and interacting with others who are going through the same issues."

Chapter 3: Revolutionary Steps to Nurture Child's Developing Mind

Everything that happens during the first five years of life can have a tremendous impact not only on how well the baby's brain is progressing right now but also on how well that baby is learning and growing over their lifetime. A reasonably straightforward matter is caring for the physical needs of your child (food, shelter, and clothing). It can be trickier to seek to provide for your child's emotional needs. While there are many types of parenting, most experts agree on some general guidelines for maintaining the emotional health of a child and laying the groundwork for emotionally healthy adulthood. Although experts say that baby brain growth is still mostly a mystery, what we know is how important a role natural parenting instinct will play in making your baby successful on the fast track. The brains of children develop quickly from birth across three ages. Growth in the brain influences all areas of development for an infant. Four main development areas exist motor (physical), language and communication, social and emotional, and cognitive. The development of the brain is a part of cognitive development. Cognitive development explains how the intelligence of a child develops, which requires the ability to think, learn, and solve problems. Such competencies impact all other developmental regions. Education and growth are essential to a child's first three years of life. Most parents are curious about how they can help develop their child's brain. The best way is to involve your child actively in everyday activities such as playing, reading, and being there when he/she is experiencing tension.

3.1 Nurturing Baby's Mind through Reading and Learning

Learning is one of the best ways to further the growth of a child's brain. The reading kick starts language and communication skills even before he/she can understand letters or words. Hearing words and seeing pictures in a child's mind binds the two. Reading the same books creates a connection between the words you say and the images on the screen. As a child grows, ask him/her to point out specific pictures on the website, such as "Where is the dog? "A lot of ways you can help, encourage, and support the growth of your child's brain as he/she grows up. The lecture is still the key to learning, with all of our modern technology. And while children and adults can learn by experimenting, reading is essential to getting an education that prepares one for life. Because of this, parents may think they need new electronic gadgets to help their kids learn necessary reading skills before school begins. All kids need, though, is their parents' time and attention, chatting, reading, singing, and playing with them. Reading and writing are like speaking on paper–the real prerequisite is developing keen language skills, including listening, speaking, and understanding what's being said. Children must also recognize and shape the forms of the letters used to represent language on paper. One essential skill is learning to understand and generate the native language's distinct sounds. That is called phonemic awareness. Infants can produce all the sounds of all the words in the world. When listening to human speech, their brain starts focusing in on the sounds of their style and imitate those sounds. The ability should train them down the road for phonics. Parents can promote the development of this essential skill with ease and pleasure by talking, reading, singing, and playing with their child. Plenty of warm and loving smiles, singing-like vocal inflections that imitate sounds, as well as touch and laughter will keep them focused so that they will learn how to distinguish between sounds and how to construct language together. Educators recommend using rhyming and clapping out the syllables of a word when reciting a short poem or singing a song to help them develop another ability known as phonological awareness (understanding how words are formed in exact order by a set of different sounds). As your child gets to understand what you're saying and reading and can interact with you through delivering a speech, you're at a point where you can build on that — ask open-ended questions about a story you're reading to your child and use a serve-and-return exchange to help them build up their vocabulary. In their own words, have your child tell the story, or make up their own. It helps them develop a new skill–understanding.

The next skill is the ability to recognize and write alphabet letters. This will allow them to develop the ability to read short letter naming beforehand. Show a message to your kids, say the word, then have them trace the letter on paper and write it in the air. You can also use clay to shape words, bend straws, or create a series of sandpaper letters for them to trace. The best way to learn this ability is through a multisensory approach– visual, auditory, kinesthetic (movement), and tactile (feeling by touch). Educators here refer to learning as the VAKT method. Recent research suggests early reader brains are using all four of the brain regions associated with each of these tasks. Most kids are ready for phonics, which is the next ability in early reading by the time they reach kindergarten. Many kids are prepared sooner, so concentrating on the first three skills above will make your kid for the early stages of learning how to read. Such three skills are best learned by regular and varying listening and engaging interactions with the human language. The way to go is not electronic gadgets, videos, computers, DVDs, and educational toys. Again, what works is for parents to talk, read, sing, and play with their kids. Such human interaction allows the child to be fully responsive to the stimuli, contributing to learning and maintaining new skills. While you and your child have fun and enjoy each other, there is also strong parent-child bonding that is essential for healthy emotional and social development.

3.2 Nurture Child's Mind through Trust, Confidence, and Love

Understanding how to trust starts at birth: babies are born entirely dependent on caregivers to fulfill their primary food, shelter, comfort, and love needs. When caregivers respond in an attentive, clear, and compassionate manner to the cries of babies and body language, these babies may feel safe and learn to trust their environment. The relationship between parent and child is the first social relationship,' Kassow says. "It teaches the child that to meet his needs, he can communicate, which transfers to form relationships later in life." From the starting age, children start to differentiate between trustworthy people and those who are not. A few researchers conducted an experiment that children aged three and four were presented with adults who had shown different names for items that the children had never seen before. Some of those names had been accurate; others had not. The four-year-olds were able to tell the exact adults from those who made lists and later searched for the honest adults, describing them as being trustworthy to the researchers. Ken Rotenberg of Keele University in the United Kingdom has found in other studies that children develop trust in response to specific experiences they have with others; this is not something they apply uniformly. "Trust is dyadic and mutual, and children have to develop unique patterns of trusting each person they meet," Rotenberg says. "So optimistic can be a disadvantage." Instead of promoting blind faith in children, Rotenberg believes that parents should focus on raising trustworthy children. "Trustworthy Children have more friends in school and are better adjusted.

Be aware of the child development stages, so you don't expect too much or too little of your child. Encourage your child to share its feelings; value those sentiments. Let your child know that pain, fear, anger, and anxiety are all felt by everyone. Try to learn the origins of those emotions. Help your child to positively express anger, without resorting to violence and promoting mutual respect and confidence. Keep your voice level down— even if you are not in agreement. Hold Channels of Communication available.

Hear out your kids. You are using words and examples that your child can understand. Foster questions. Provide convenience and assurance. Be frank. Concentrate on the positive. Express your willingness to discuss any subject. Look at your skills in problem-solving and coping. Do you set a good example? If you are frustrated by the feelings or actions of your infant, or if you cannot control your frustration or rage, seek help. Encourage the strengths of your kids and recognize limitations. Set goals based on the talents and desires of the child— not the expectations of another. Feast on successes. Do not compare your child's abilities to those of other kids; appreciate your child's uniqueness. Pass time with your child regularly. Foster independence and self-worth for your child. Help your child tackle the ups and downs in life. Express confidence in the ability of your child to manage challenges, and address new experiences. Discipline with constructiveness, fairness, and consistency. Using training as an instructional tool and not as physical punishment. All kids and families are different; learn what works for your kid. Express support for positive behaviors. Help your child learn from its mistakes. Give unconditional love to your child. Teach others the importance of excuses, cooperation, tolerance, empathy, and consideration. Don't expect perfectness; parenting is a tough job.

A good relationship is built on confidence, security, and love. Taking advantage of these three principles is essential to a healthy relationship with your teenager. Even though your child is getting more participative in her peer relationships, it is still vital for you to be attentive to her needs and be there to direct and help her. Parents are considered the first teacher of their child, and their relationship with her forms the cornerstone of its emotional and social growth.

Reset standards and limits. Take out some time and have a conversation with your child about your values, rules, and expectations regularly and the reasons behind them helps give her a blueprint of proper behavior. You can start doing this by explaining your household rules and ensuring you are consistently adhering to them. For starters, curfew during the middle-school years is becoming a big issue. It is significant to describe the reasons why you set this specific curfew time to your child and discuss the implications of failing to meet this deadline. If she violates her curfew, be sure to follow through and let her bear through the results and outcomes, as this can be helpful for her in developing a sense of responsibility and accountability. The same goes for expectations relating to the school. When she fails to take an exam, ask her what happened. Allow her to articulate her reasons for her acts and help her understand how she can change such habits, such as through timely analysis of more or completing homework. Try making these interactions as healthy as possible, and at the moment. Middle-schoolers have a meager moral ability to lecture.

The most crucial primary foundation for both intellectual and social growth is to nurture emotional relationships. Relationships cultivate comfort, affection, and enjoyment at the most basic level; furnish security, physical safety, and disease and injury protection; and provide basic nutritional and housing needs. Relationship "regulatory" factors (for example, protecting children from over-or under-stimulation) help children stay calm and alert for new learning. When relationships are secure, empathetic, nurturing, children learn to be intimate and empathetic, and ultimately communicate their feelings, reflect on their desires and develop their relationships. Relationships also teach children which actions are and which are not acceptable. As the behavior of children in the second year of life becomes more nuanced, they know from the facial expressions, tone of voice, movements, and vocabulary of their careers what kind of behavior contributes to approval or disapproval. Patterns are built up between children and careers by giving-and-taking. But emotions, wishes, and self-image also come into being along with behavior. For relationships, the emotional tone and implicit gestures are essential to who we are and what we lean.

3.3 Twelve Innovative Strategies to Nurture Child's Brain

A few complicated parts of the brain (prefrontal cortex) are still under development during childhood and adolescence. This side of the brain is responsible for higher-order and analytical thinking and is not developed until a person reaches the mid-twenties. Conversely, the "Downstairs Brain" (one part of which is the Amygdala) is responsible for rapid processing. This side of the brain is more primitive and lets us act before we think in hazardous situations, which require a faster response.

1) "Connect and Redirect: Surfing Emotional Waves" If your child is upset, it's important to connect first using both your right brains to make an emotional connection and let them know you're upset, even if your child doesn't fully understand the' why' behind it. Then, once your child has more control and is more receptive, you can bring the left brain into this discussion to talk about any lessons, subjects, and discipline that need to be discussed.

2) "Call It to Tame It: Telling Stories to Calm Large Emotions": It can be good to talk about experiences. Experience telling and retelling can help calm down big right-brain feelings

and emotions because the left brain can help and assist in making sense of the experiences and helping make your child feel more in control.

3) "Engage, Don't Enrage: Talk to the Upstairs Brain": In cases where emotions are high, allowing your child to reach the parts of their "Upstairs Brain" that are available to them. Rather than activating the more simplistic "Downstairs Brain" will help engage your child in the process of finding solutions. Be curious by asking questions that provide options/alternatives and use this as an opportunity to exercise negotiating skills.

4) "Use It or Lose It: Upstairs Brain": helping your child grow their "Upstairs Brain" while under construction will help build neural pathways, and the process of reaching those pathways helps to build stronger connections in the future time and time again. Creating a game, "What'd you do?" It can be a great practice to let your child discuss and think about a range of approaches to different issues. While it may be appealing for us to share our own ideas/thought, try not to rescue children from difficult decisions, as it does not provide the same experience as when exercising their "Brain Upstairs."

5) "Move It or Lose It: Movement in the Body to Avoid Losing the Mind: "One of the best things we can do when a child has lost contact with its" Upstairs Brain "is to help them recover their equilibrium by moving their body. Studies have shown that our emotional state (i.e., our mood) can be improved by exercise (e.g., going for a walk or running) or relaxation (e.g., deep breathing, yoga) by our physical state.

6) "Use the Remote of Mind: Replaying Memories: Children never have the opportunity to be in charge of much of what is going on in their lives, and so when they have the opportunity to do so, it can be a great learning experience for them. Children can often be reluctant to talk about painful events/memories. Using a figurative remote that allows them to' stop," rewind,' and' fast-forward' sections of the story will help them feel in control of what they want to say then and encourage them to work up to the more challenging information to speak about.

7) "Remember: Make Recollection a Part of the Daily Life of Your Family": Another essential way to help exercise the brain of your child is to help them use the power of remembering. Thinking of significant past events helps to reconcile memories that are subconscious and clear. The simple act of giving children a chance to tell their stories helps them to understand their past and present experiences better.

8) "Let the Clouds of Feelings Roll by Learning That Feelings Come and Go": Teaching children that feelings are like clouds that come and go, and letting them roll by helping them understand that these are fleeting states rather than permanent features. It is significant to differentiate between "feel" and "am."

9) Giving attention to what's going on inside: making your kids pay attention to the "Sensations, Pictures, Feelings and Thoughts" that exist within them is an excellent way to make them aware of what they experience. This is the first vital piece to help your kids develop "Mindsight," which is the awareness of our minds as well as others' thoughts.

10) "Exercise' Mindsight': Getting back to the Hub": the "Wheel of Perception" is a device that can allow us to imagine our mind like a bike wheel complete with an outer rim, spokes, and an inner hub. Our emotions, feelings, visions, memories, perceptions, and body sensations are on the wheel's outer edge, and the center hub is the place where our consciousness resides, this is the location from where we can choose the point on which we want to concentrate (the spokes, see below). Kids, like adults, can find themselves stuck in a particular thought and can help them gain more control over how they feel, showing them that they can shift their attention and focus on another idea. The method of "mindsight" helps kids learn how to relax and focus their attention on where they want it to be.

11) "Improve Family Fun Factor: Making a Point for Enjoying Every Other": many parents/caregivers frequently discover that they invest so much of their time either disciplining their children and going from one activity to another. "Playful Parenting" (for example, being dumb, telling jokes or playing games) is one way you can create healthy relationships with your kids. This encourages children to have positive experiences with their parents/caregivers and also helps to model future relationships and relationships.

12) "Connecting via Conflict: Teaching children to disagree with a' We' in Mind': Conflict is often seen as something to be get rid at all costs, but it is not realistic or necessary. Teaching our children how to use Mindsight's power to handle the dispute in healthy, creative ways can be an excellent learning opportunity to build skills such as taking the perspective of another person, reading non-verbal indications, and making corrections.

3.4 Research Study on Nurturing Child's Brain through Mother's Love

Feeding a child early in life may help him or her grow a greater hippocampus, a new study shows the brain region that is important for learning, memory and stress responses. Previous animal research has shown that early maternal support has a positive effect on hippocampal development, brain cell production, and the ability to deal with stress in a young rat. On the other hand, research in human children found a link between early social experiences and the volume of the Amygdala, which helps to regulate the production and memory of emotional reactions. Numerous studies have also found that children born in a nursing setting usually perform better at school and are more socially mature than their peers who have not been nursed. Brain scans have now shown that love for a mother physically influences the hippocampus volume of her brain. Kids of nursing mothers had 10 percent greater hippocampal volumes in the sample than kids whose mothers were not as nursing. We can now confidently say that the psychosocial climate is having a significant impact on the way the human brain grows. Research is a part of ongoing process. This puts a mighty wind behind the sail of the notion that early childcare has a positive effect on their development. Children with rapid onset depression development.

3.5 Nurturing Child's Imagination

More than narrating a story or painting a picture, a child who is particularly creative excels. Research studies show that innovative and creative people who work in the sciences and the arts can better perceive what others might think or feel, can see problems from different points of view, and have superior self-control (probably because they can formulate multiple results to a problem). The Academy of Pediatrics, situated in America, now suggests that doctors "prescribe" a certain amount of solo play to spur inventive thinking every day. All the kids can and should learn to tap their creativity. Early breastfeeding, the creative side of your child spills into other areas of your life. A kid who is motivated to think out of the box will be able to search for new and innovative problems solutions. Flexible and creative thinking has become critical to success in school, at work, and in life in our dynamic, fast-paced world. Toddlerhood, as it happens, is a perfect time to focus on imagination because, by definition, it is the most creative phase of a child's life. Two-year-Old only have a poor idea of what's real and fictional. Imagining out of the box is easy because the box's limitations have not yet been met. Nothing seems unlikely for them. A 4-year-old who wants a high counter cookie will likely get out a chair to stand on–a strategy she knows is successful. In comparison, a toddler could pile up her stuffed animals to climb on or try to jump up and down to the counter. She has to invent her ideas because she can't yet understand what works and what doesn't.

Guidelines for Nurturing Child's Creativity

- **Encourage aggressive pursuits, not passive ones.**

Speak of creativity as a muscle: it will atrophy if it is not exercised. Kids involved in passive behaviors, such as watching TV, take pictures and ideas from other people rather than coming up with their own, says Jane M. Healy, Ph.D., an educational psychologist and author of Failure to Link (Simon & Schuster, 1998). Ordinary experiences like reading aloud or walking outside do much more than television to grow the creative side of a brain, she says. Commit the 2-year-old to the conversation as often as possible. Ask questions that inspire him to share his ideas and thoughts. Tell him stories and let him deliver the ending–or better yet, a range of finishes.

- **Provide plenty of safe deliveries.**

Toddlers love exploring new ways to use stuff, so search for non-toxic finger-paints, markers, and clays and play dough that is harmless when consumed. Dress-up clothes and hats should be comfortable to get on and off, free of anything that might trap or choke a child. No hard edges or thin, detachable pieces should be present in the musical instruments.

- **Let them make choices for your kids.**

Each time it's convenient (and safe), let your child think for himself. Wonder if she wants to drink from the green cup or the blue cup, for example, or if he likes to wear the striped pants or the plaid ones. Although such options may seem trivial to an adult, they will be considered thrilling by a child who is starting to acquire self-control over her life.

- **Tolerate uncertainty.**

If your child is engaging in creative play, resign yourself to chaos and resist such phrases as "That's too messy" or "That's not going there. Normally she is very reluctant to do anything that isn't completely organized." Participate in creative projects.

Research has shown that children whose parents are interested in imaginative play to develop more extensive vocabulary and more versatile thinking skills. So, sit down with your kid and paint his palm. Or get him to play dress-up. "If you're interested, he'll be interested too.

- **Know precisely what to expect.**

To think a kid would draw a recognizable picture of a house or tell a story with a comprehensible start, middle and end are unrealistic. What you can expect. Don't pressure your baby into making things that look like the real equivalent or sound like that. Praise everything, he makes, even if to you it seems like a page full of scriptable. You can also display the artwork of your child in the fridge or above your desk.

- **Don't push them.**

Never demand that a child get involved in creative ventures unless he's interested. And realize that his attention can dwindle rapidly, even if he is. Above all, you want your child to know that it's a joy to savor the creative process and not a burden to endure.

Chapter 4: Changes in Brain

Neuroplasticity, also term as brain plasticity, neuroplasticity, or neural plasticity, is the brain's ability to change regularly throughout an individual's life. For instance, brain activity associated with a given task can be a move to a different location, the proportion of gray matter can change, and synapses can strengthen or weaken over time. Neuroplasticity is aimed at improving neural networks during phylogenesis, ontogeny, and physiological development, as well as after a brain injury. Studies in the latter half of the 20th century have shown that even after adulthood, many parts of the brain may be changed (or are "plastic." The developing brain does, however, show a higher degree of plasticity than the adult brain. This process is called "brain plasticity"— as we experience the world, develop behaviors, and learn new knowledge, our minds alter, new connections grow, and damaged one's repair. Our experiences and expertise keep our brains functioning, developing, and learning as we age. You may experience significant changes, but not all of them are a sign of concern. We always lose our keys and forget the names of the people. We do it through our lives. It's not until we're older than we get worried about these common mishaps. It is also significant to acquire knowledge that there are several other reasons why memory lapses occur, such as taking certain medicines, lack of sleep, and excessive alcohol.

Neuroplasticity can be observed on various scales, ranging from microscopic changes in individual neurons to larger-scale changes such as cortical regeneration in response to injury.

Behavior, environmental stimuli, thought, and emotions can also induce neuroplastic transform by the help of activity-dependent plasticity, which has significant implications for healthy development, learning, memory, and bra recovery. Synaptic plasticity directs to alterations in the connections between neurons at the single-cell level. In contrast, non-synaptic flexibility relates to changes in their intrinsic excitability.

4.1 Research and Discovery of Neuroplasticity

In 1923, Karl Lashley, scientist, conducted experiments on rhesus monkeys showing changes in neuronal pathways, which he concluded were plasticity proof. Neuroscientists have not generally accepted the idea of neuroplasticity, despite this, and other work that indicated plasticity.

In 1945, another scientist Justo Gonzalo concluded from his research on brain dynamics that, opposite to the movement of the projection areas, the "central" cortical mass (more or less equidistant from the visual, tactile and auditory projection areas) would be a rather unspecified or multisensory "maneuvering mass" with the ability to increase neural excitability and reorganize activity through plasticity. Another scientist provided the first scientific evidence of anatomical brain plasticity, publishing her work in 1964.

Other relevant proof was produced in the 1960s and after that, especially from scientists including Paul Bach-y-Rita, Michael Merzenich, along with Jon Kaas and many others. In the 1960s, Paul Bach-y-Rita invented a device that was tested on a small number of people and involved a person sitting in a chair with fixed nubs that were made to vibrate in ways that translated images received in the camera, allowing for a form of vision through sensory substitution.

Eleanor Maguire reported improvements in the hippocampal structure associated with gaining local taxi drivers' knowledge of London's style.

In London Taxi Drivers, a redistribution of gray matter was reported as compared to controls. Not only interested scientists were involved in this research on hippocampal plasticity but also engaged the public and media around the world.

Michael Merzenich is a neuroscientist who pioneered neuroplasticity for more than three decades. He made some of the "most ambitious claims for the field–that brain exercises can be as useful as drugs for treating sickness as chronic as schizophrenia. That plasticity exists from the cradle to the grave, and that radical improvement in cognitive functioning–how we can learn, think, perceive, and remember even in the elderly. Neuroplasticity may occur beyond the critical period. However, Merzenich argued. His first experience with adult plasticity came when he worked with Clinton Woosley is a postdoctoral study. The experiment was based on an investigation of what has happened in the brain while cutting and then regenerating one peripheral nerve. Before and after trimming a peripheral nerve and stitching the ends together, the two scientists micromapped the hand maps of monkey brains. The hand map in the mind which they expected to be jumbled afterward was almost normal. That was a significant development. Merzenich argued that "If the brain map was able to normalize its structure in response to an abnormal input, the prevailing view that we were born with a hardwired mechanism must be incorrect.

Types of Neuroplasticity

As described above by Shaw and McEachern, in the study of neuroplasticity, there is no all-inclusive theory that overshoots different frameworks and systems.

Researchers, however, often describe neuroplasticity as "the ability to make adaptive changes related to the nervous system's structure and function.

Two types of neuroplasticity are frequently discussed accordingly: structural neuroplasticity and functional neuroplasticity.

Structural Neuroplasticity

Structural plasticity is often comprehended as the capacity of the brain to alter its neuronal connections. Depending on this form of neuroplasticity, new neurons are continually generated and inserted into the central nervous system over the entire life cycle. Scientists now use multiple cross-sectional imaging techniques (i.e., magnetic resonance imaging (MRI), computerized tomography (CT)) to study human brain structural changes. This type of neuroplasticity also studies the effects of various internal or external stimuli on the anatomical reorganization of the brain. The shifts in the proportion of grey matter or the synaptic intensity in mind are known as manifestations of central neuroplasticity. In current academic, structural neuroplasticity is being investigated more in the field of neuroscience.

Functional neuroplasticity

Functional plasticity (also called synaptic plasticity) refers to the capacity of the brain to modify and change the neuronal communication. The changes often occur because of, but not limited to, neuron dysfunction or damage; functions from one part of the brain move to another part of the brain based on the need for recovery of behavioral or physiological processes. (LTP) Long-term potentiation and long-term depression (LTD) are known as examples of memory-related synaptic plasticity.

4.2 How Brain Changes with Age

As with the rest of your body, with each year, your brain changes. The minds have evolved from the time we are children, studying, making memories, and more. We become wiser and stronger.

We receive the knowledge that only comes with the experience of life. Of course, the less desirable effects of the time mark can also be felt. You should recognize them: an ever-lost set of keys, a to-do that never seems to remain top of mind, a name on your tongue's tip. When we reach our late 20s, the aging process of the brain begins, and we begin to lose neurons — the cells that make up the brain and nervous system. Our minds had practically started to shrink by our sixties. Though these changes in the brain may sound a bit frightening, the process is normal, and it happens to all. Learn how the brain evolves as you age to get better grip on what's going on in this magical part of your body. Then, have a glance at some of the things you can do to help preserve brain health. Although some change is inevitable, a healthy lifestyle will ward some off. Here's how you can participate in playing an active role in slowing down adverse effects and striving towards better, more extended stays.

You're born with necessary survival skills, reflexes, and most of the 100 billion neurons you're going to have for the lifetime. During these early years, the brain grows remarkably rapidly: Neurons grow bigger, work more efficiently, and, as a result of environmental inputs and stimuli, make trillions of connections that fine-tune everything from hearing to vision. The brain is around 80 percent of its adult size by the age of two. About 85 percent of brain development, including intellect, personality, and motor and social skills, has occurred by now. The brain of an infant has twice that number of synapses as the brain of an adult. In a process called pruning, neural links that are most often used and strengthened — those that are used for language — are reinforced, while those that are not used so much fizzle and die. The character has set out like plaster in most of us, by the age of thirty, and will never soften again. The aim is to continually create new pathways and connections to break apart neuronal structures that are trapped in the brain.

Simply put, there is a lot of flexibility and plasticity when the brain is young and not yet fully formed, which explains why children learn so quickly. It concluded that we, as human beings, grow neural pathways, and the more over the years and years we use these neural pathways, they become much trapped and deeply embedded, going into deeper portions of the brain. As we reach the age of 25, we have just so many developed pathways on which our brain depends. It's hard to break free from them. One explanation is that our mind is inherently lazy and will always choose the most energy-efficient path if we allow it. If you want to keep your brain productive and healthy, you'll need to zero in on areas of your mind that you're using less often. And this new exercise has to be so severe that after you complete the job, you will feel mentally and physically tired because you are pushing your brain to work in the ways it is uncommon. Only in this manner can you grow new neurons powerful enough to interact with existing neurons, creating new pathways.

Depression Causes Brain to age faster – A Research Study

New research from Yale University suggests that stress can physically change the brain of a person, hurrying an aging effect that could make them more susceptible to old age-related diseases. In this past, scientists have found manner of evidence to show depression affects the brain and other parts of the body.

The disorder has been associated with, among other things, an increased risk of headaches, muscle pains, and sleep problems. And it can develop a negative feedback loop: a study published in the Journal of Clinical Psychology in 2004 found that "the worse the painful physical symptoms, the more severe the depression is." With that in mind, Irina Esterlis, a researcher at the Yale School of Medicine, placed out to learn more specifically about how depression affects the brain.

At the American Association for the Advancement of Science Conference in Washington DC, she discussed her findings on Feb. 14. Her research was based on a new kind of brain-imaging technology that gives doctors better insight into what's going on inside the brains of people. Usually, she works from a Yale laboratory where she experiments with sophisticated positron emission tomography (PET) scanners that can identify biochemical changes in body tissues. In this case, Esterlis analyzed the brains of 20 people—10 diagnosed with clinical depression and ten considered stable after completing a rigorous psychiatric evaluation — and found that those with more severe depression symptoms had lower synaptic density in the brains. Synaptic density is essential since synapses are mostly tiny bridges that rely on nerve cells to pass their impulses from cell to cell. Neurological disorders have been associated with a loss of synapses, and it is shared in people aged 74 to 90. All this to conclude, Esterlis' research suggests that that aging by-product was apparent in people with depression. To be sure, it's a small study, but the outcome was convincing enough to potentially prompt new research into what's happening to the brain when a person is anxious and depressed. Researchers at the University of Toronto are working on a drug that seems capable of preventing memory loss associated with depression and aging. According to the Financial Times (paywall), the scientists behind that research have introduced themselves at the conference in DC. The work is still in its early stages— only being conducted on mice— but it could wind up solving the very question Esterlis is uncovering in work.

Improved Functioning of Brain with Aging

We are watching younger colleague's quickly master new computer systems or pull all-nights out of place with nary a hair and — quite naturally— we're concerned.

Thankfully, modern brain science research suggests that maybe we should be less fretting. Neuroscientists have begun to home in on the changes in the brain in the middle age over the past few years, and what they have discovered is promising. Long-term studies results show that — contrary to myths — we are growing smarter in key middle-age areas that now range from our mid-40s to our mid-60s, with longer life spans. The brains function better than they did in the 20s, in fields as diverse as language and inductive reasoning. As we get older, we get the "gist" of claims more quickly. It even strengthens our assessment of others. Also, we literally "know" whether to trust someone — or some concept. We're all getting better at knowing what to ignore and when to hold our tongues. Not long ago, a mid-level executive told his colleague how the way he interacts with younger colleagues he'd recently changed. He keeps his "mouth shut" and listens when he has gathered to address a question. Even though he has the right solution— more often than not— he awaits. He is not thinking. Indeed, although he did not realize it, the executive used the best pieces of his peaceful and more experienced middle-aged brain to help him manage his situation— and achieve better results. Our minds will indeed show a bit of fraying by midlife. The speed of brain processing is slowing down. We often cannot master it as fastly as our younger peers in the face of new knowledge. And there is little question which our short-term memories are suffering from. When you find that you can't think back to the name of that person you know in the elevator or even the movie you saw last week, it's easy to panic. But it turns out that those abilities don't matter that much. Our minds have built a whole host of talents by midlife that is just as well suited to managing the new, dynamic workplace. As we age, we get to see the possible better. Predictably, younger minds are set up to focus on the negative and future issues. Studies show that older brains frequently find solutions faster, in part because they concentrate on what can be achieved. By the time we arrive middle age, millions of patterns have been formed in our brains, and those linked pathways provide invaluable perspective— even when it's subconscious.

4.3 What Happens to Brain as we Age

It has been commonly observed that the volume of the brain and its weight decreases with age at a speed of around 5 percent per decade after period 401, with the actual price of drop likely to increase with age, especially over period 70.2. How this occurs is less clear. Shrinking gray matter is often reported to have been caused by neuronal cell death, but it is not entirely clear whether this is solely responsible or even the primary finding. It has been suggested that a decline in neuronal volume rather than number contributes to changes in an aging brain and may be related to sex with different areas most affected by men and women.

Additionally, the dendritic arbor, spines, and synapses can alter. Therefore, dendritic sprouting can occur, maintaining a similar number of synapses5 and compensating for any cell death. Four conversely, a decrease in dendritic synapses or loss of synaptic plasticity has also been described. Functional organizational change can occur and compensate similarly to that found in patients after recovery from moderate traumatic brain injury. However, latte research has been conducted. We also need to think about the role of white matter in the aging brain. White matter can decline with age, myelin sheath may deteriorate even in healthy aging after about 40 years of age, and it has been reported that the late myelinating regions of the frontal lobes are most influenced by white matter lesions (WML). However, not all studies support this view. Leukoaraiosis / WML increases with age and may suggest ischemia in subclinical cases. They'll be covered in the more fabulous description below.

Brain alteration does not occur to an identical degree in all brain regions. A longitudinal study supports the fact that these brain changes are not consistent, using two MRI scans separated by about one to two years, and a cross-sectional research examination. The latter included only those research that contrasted younger (under 30 years of age) and older (over 60) groups to compare broader age ranges and in comparison to much of the other work in this area. The study looked at range and found the most affected was the prefrontal cortex. With the survey covering over seven tests, the striatum came in second. The temporal lobe, cerebellar vermis, cerebellar hemispheres, and hippocampus also decrease volume with between 8 and 18 studies and also showed a reduction in prefrontal white matter (five reviews). The occipital cortex was the last one to be affected (five studies). The result that the prefrontal cortex is most affected, and the occipital least, matches well with the cognitive changes seen during aging. However, some studies do indicate that aging has the most significant effect in the hippocampus. Men and women may also vary as opposed to the hippocampus and parietal lobes in women with frontal and temporal lobes most impact on men. Finally, the rate of brain volume reduction may increase, especially over 70 years of age, although the number studied is minimal. Due to the individual differences in brain growth and aging mapping structure to function and change due to aging is a complicated task. Still, there are studies showing connections between volume and neuropsychological function. A study examining the amount of cortical volume and white matter hyperintensity in 140 people between the ages of 50 and 81 pre-screened for dementia and depression found an association between increased ages, decreased prefrontal cortical volume, increased subcortical white matter lesions, and increased perseverance (decreased executive function).

Cognitive Change

The most frequently observed cognitive change associated with aging is memory. Memory function can be commonly split into four parts, episodic memory, semantic memory, procedural memory, and working memory. In terms of aging, the first two of these are most relevant. Episodic memory is described as type of memory where information is stored with' mental tags,' where, when, and how it was collected." An example of episodic memory would be a retention of your first school day, the critical meeting you attended last week, or the lesson you learned that Paris is France's capital. The performance of episodic memory is thought to decline from middle age on. This is specifically true in the case of recall during healthy aging and less so for identification. It is also a symptom of memory loss found in Alzheimer's disease (AD). Semantic memory is defined, for example, as "memory for meanings," knowing that Paris is France's capital, that 10 millimeters make up one centimeter, or that Mozart composed the Magic Flute. Semantic memory gradually increases from middle age to young, older adults but then declines in the very elderly. It is not yet understood why these alterations happen, and it has been hypothesized that the very elderly have fewer resources to draw on and that their performance may be affected by slower reaction times. Lower attention levels, slower processing speeds, detrimental sensory and perceptual functions, or potentially less ability to use strategies in specific tasks. Studies have been conducted using neuropsychological testing and neuroimaging to explore different types of memory in aging.

Nevertheless, it must be pointed out that some of these features, such as episodic memory encoding and semantic memory retrieval, are sometimes methodologically difficult to separate. Notwithstanding, these experiments of aging and neuroimaging are starting to investigate success on memory tasks.

A review article focused on this area illustrated improvements in the activation of regional brains. Older brains tend to show more symmetrical activation, either because they have raised activation in a less activated hemisphere than in younger adults, or because they have reduced activation in the most activated areas of younger adults. It has been shown in memory tasks and for visual perception. The observed changes inactivation in the prefrontal left and right cortex are in line with alterations in the performance of the memory, particularly episodic memory, as this is thought to be centered in this region. It has also been proposed that the actual brain stimulation level, as shown in neuroimaging, may be more directly related to the memory performance levels. A research analysis using electroencephalograms to analyze event-related potentials in response to stimuli also provides some evidence for the improved similarity of age-related brain activation. The increased symmetric hemispheric activation in older adults is a reliable finding and has been referred to as HAROLD or reduction in hemispheric asymmetry. It is not understood whether this shift is the attention of the response seen in younger participants, an inability to recruit specific areas, or an effort to compensate for the aging process. Nevertheless, this increase in activation occurring in the frontal lobes matches with improvements in memory performance and the possible changes in the white matter listed above, but other factors such as changes in neurocranium.

Mechanism Changes

The most often addressed neurotransmitters as regards aging are dopamine and serotonin.

Dopamine levels are decreasing by about 10 percent per decade from early adulthood and have been associated with cognitive and motor function declines. It may be that the dopaminergic pathways between the frontal cortex and the striatum decrease with increasing age, or that dopamine levels themselves decrease, synapses/receptors decrease, or that binding receptor decrease. Neurotrophic factor levels derived from serotonin and brain often drop with increasing age and may be involved in controlling synaptic plasticity and neurogenesis in the adult brain. A neurotransmitter-related product, monoamine oxidase, increases with age and can release free radicals from reactions that surpass the endogenous antioxidant reserves. Other factors involved in the aging brain include calcium dysregulation, mitochondrial dysfunction, and reactive oxygen species production. The hormonal effect is another factor to consider about the developing brain and its cognitive performance. It is known that sex hormones can influence cognitive processes in adulthood, and changes in sex hormones occur during aging, particularly in menopause women. Females also have a higher incidence of AD, even when given more extended life expectancy. AD is characterized by memory loss, and suggestions have been made that estrogen therapy can increase dopaminergic reactivity and play a protective part in AD. It should be recalled, however, that recent use of HRT has been shown to pose cancer risks. Growth hormone levels often decline with age and may be correlated with cognitive performance even though the evidence is far from conclusive. The aging brain may also suffer from decreased glucose metabolism or diminished glucose or oxygen intake, as cerebrovascular effectiveness declines. In contrast, glucose loss may be partially due to atrophy rather than any improvement in the metabolism of glucose. Change in the vasculature is significant, and ischemia-related white matter lesions and stroke are other common findings in older brains.

Vascular Factors

For rising age, WML, strokes, and dementia increase. WML shows heritability levels are reasonable in the elderly, even when asymptomatic and are not the innocuous finding they were once considered to be.

For a summary, see Hsu-Ko.42 WML or hyperintensities are related to increased cardiovascular risk and decreased cerebral blood flow, cerebral reactivity, and vascular density. However, it is uncertain whether the WML causes loss of vessels or vice versa.

When using magnetization shift magnetic resonance imaging, they may also be correlated with further tissue shifts in visible grey matter.

WML is found more in frontal rather than posterior brain regions in line with the cognitive and morphological findings discussed above) and it has been shown that WML is related to poor cognition. Other damages associated with aging and blood pressure and vascular factors include strokes and small vessel disease. Moderate to high outpatient blood pressure 24 hours was associated with increased brain atrophy, as the amplitude of systolic blood pressure increased.

In Japanese subjects, elevated systolic blood pressure was correlated with loss of grey matter volume in a cross-sectional analysis, and an increased 10-year risk of the first stroke was associated with declines in cognitive function in the Framingham offspring cohort. The authors recommend that this may be attributable to cerebrovascular-related injuries, progressive atrophy, white matter disorders, or asymptomatic infarction.

The fact that cerebral vasculature may be associated with cognitive function is not surprising, as microvasculature's ability to respond to metabolic demand declines with increasing age, and functional adult neurogenesis may also be correlated with good metabolic demand. See Lie et al. for reviews, and Riddle et al. Besides this, many links have been made between dementia, even AD, and risk factors for vascular disease. Increasing evidence points to vascular factors contributing not only to aging cognitive issues but also to the two most common dementias seen in the people. The happening of dementia rises almost exponentially, with about 20 percent of those aged 80 affected rising to 40 percent of those aged 90.39 The most commonly observed forms of dementia in the elderly are AD, which accounts for about 40 percent –70 percent of dementias, and vascular dementia (VaD) has risen to 15 percent –30 percent. A postmortem study found that 77 percent of VaD cases showed AD pathology60, and high blood pressure was associated with increased AD characteristic neurofibrillary tangles. Several forms of vascular disease have been related to AD, including microvascular degeneration, blood-brain barrier disorders, WML, microinfarction, and cerebral hemorrhage. Significant vessel causes, such as atherosclerosis, have been suggested to increase the risk of AD and may play a role in the amyloid deposition of the cerebral vessel. AD patients show significantly higher levels of cerebrovascular pathology compared to postmortem examination controls, although this did not correlate with cognitive decline severity. The same research finding resulted that small infarcts in AD do not affect the rate of cognitive decline, suggests that vascular factors may unmask or magnify the underlying AD pathology, or lowered the pre-clinical phase of AD, at least in Western populations. At postmortem examination, the characteristic neurofibrillary tangles and plaques found in AD are also evident to some extent in most elderly brains, even those without symptoms, as are white matter lesions. The issue of healthy aging is complicated because studies are showing cognitively intact adults aged and yet an increasing percentage suffer from dementia and the line between mild cognitive ages. Without question, changes in brain vasculature, WML, and intra / extracellular changes are likely to begin in midlife. There are many factors on the aging brain, biology, biological, and environmental influences, all leading to physiological and cognitive changes. Mattson gave it a review.

Risk factors proposed in terms of aging and dementia development include hypertension, diabetes, hyperhomocysteinemia, and high cholesterol, although evidence for all but hypertension is far from conclusive. Safeguarding factors include diet, alcohol, exercise, and intellectual pursuits.

4.4 Aging Slows down the Brain

Processing speed means just that to a brain scientist: the pace at which a person can take in a bit of new knowledge, make some conclusion on it and then formulate a response. Studies suggest that the speed of information processing varies with age along an inverted U-shaped curve, such that our learning accelerates from childhood to adolescence, retains a period of relative stability leading to middle age, and then, slowly but steadily decreases in late middle age and onward.

It is usual for most people to see that processing speed slows with age.

Many older adults had noticed they take longer to solve problems or make decisions than they did when they were young. Yet the explanations for this age-related deceleration in the processing of information are not fully understood and can vary from person to person.

Some compelling evidence indicates that such a deterioration represents wear and tear of white brain matter, which consists of all the wires or axons that link one part of the brain to another. Slowed transmission of information along axons can hinder processing speed. But what initially causes the axonal contact to slow down? Diabetes, smoking, high blood pressure, or other so-called vascular risk factors in some people can wear away at the blood vessels feeding the white matter of the brain, starving axons of much-needed oxygen and glucose. Many individuals may have a genetic predisposition to decay of white matter related to age, a theory that is poorly understood but has been extensively studied. Slowed processing rate could be the first indicator of neurodegenerative disease in other people, such as Alzheimer's disease. Head trauma may play a role, including concussions. These are just a few of the many ideas out there — other factors certainly still to be discovered. Most specifically, slow processing of information affects almost every aging person to some extent, and the distinction between natural and abnormal becomes blurred. By paying close attention to vascular risk factors, participating in daily aerobic exercise, eating well, and continuing to challenge oneself mentally, a person may maintain or even increase the speed of information processing.

Think achy joints are the main reason we're slowing down as we age? But blame the brain: The portion responsible for movement will start a slow downhill slide at age 40. How easily you can throw a ball, or sprint or turn a steering wheel depends on how quickly brain cells fire off muscle commands. Fast firing is dependent on good insulation for cabling your brain. Now new research suggests that even stable people in middle age begin to lose some of that insulation in a section of the brain's motor-control — at the same time as their speed slows slowly. This helps explain why it's hard after 40, to be a world-class athlete.

Research Study

Stuff starts going south at age 24, according to researchers at Simon Fraser University in Canada. Since researching 3,305 volunteers aged 16 years to 44 years, they came to that conclusion. The participants played a real-time game that approximated real-world situations of everyday life that test our cognitive abilities, from attention to juggling multiple tasks to changing our emphasis from immediate to long-term problems. The game captured moves from the players, and researchers were analyzing hours of data from it. The pace with which the volunteers made decisions, and moved between tasks, declined with age as planned. Several studies have recorded an increasing loss of cognitive competencies over time. But in this report, published in the PLOS One journal, the drop was first observed among 24-year-olds, although tiny. Cognitive speed dropped by about 15 percent every 15 years after age 24. And the results could not be explained by the fact that, over time, the players were getting better at navigating the game; the age-related decline remained, even among those with more skill playing the play. This doesn't mean everything is downhill until your mid-20s. When processing speed slows, the brain compensates for some of the loss in a variety of ways. For instance, by relying on experience to foresee and predict future activities more accurately, as well as by using mental shortcuts such as removing foreign information and stopping incoming information into only core nuggets of relevant material. And while we might get slower, we might get smarter, too.

4.5 Effects of Aging Brain on Thinking

The brain controls many facets of thinking — remembering, planning, arranging, decision-making, and more. Such cognitive skills influence how well we do our daily tasks and whether we can live independently.

Aging can bring about positive cognitive improvements, too. Those from a lifetime of experiences often have more knowledge and insight. As a person grows older, changes are taking place in all parts of the body, including the brain. Some parts of the brain shrink, especially those that are necessary for learning and other complex mental activities. Communication between the neurons (nerve cells) may be reduced in specific brain regions. Blood flow can decrease in the brain, too. Inflammation may increase, which occurs when the body responds to an injury or disease.

Such brain changes can impair mental function, even in stable older persons. For example, some older adults find that complex memory or learning tests do not do as well as younger people. And they can do as well, given enough time. There is increasing evidence that, as people age, the brain remains "plastic" — capable of adapting to new challenges and tasks.

It is not understood why some people think well while others do not. One possible reason is the "cognitive reserve," the ability of the brain to function well even when a part of it is disrupted. Those with more experience tend to have a higher amount of memory than others. Many changes in the brain, such as those linked to Alzheimer's disease, are not a standard part of aging.

It's irritating, but it's sadly true: most parts of the bodywork less well as one gets older. This is the fact of the brain, which is part of why having a "tip of the tongue" moment becomes more regular as one gets older.

These age-related changes are called "cognitive aging," in how the brain regulates memory, thought, and other mental processes. Understanding how aging affects cognition is crucial. It can help you to understand what to expect when it comes to aging yourself.

It can also help families better understand the alterations they observe in an older person, and whether or not those changes are out of the ordinary. As you will see, over time, most mental processes get less agile. Just as your 75-year-old self cannot run as fast as your 30-year-old self, so, for the most part, your 75-year-old brain will not think as quickly either. To many people, this can be disappointing news. What does it mean they might feel hesitant to know more about this? But they're not just bad news. Sure, things tend to work a little slower and less well, but by relying on their experience, older adults can often compensate. When I clarify later in the article, cognitive aging often helps older adults become more positive and emotionally resilient. You'll be better provided to comprehend the older adults in your life by better understanding cognitive aging, whether it's yourself or an older loved one.

People often think about memory when they talk about learning or "brain function," but there's a lot more to think about and the functioning of the brain. Here are six key ways in which aging affects cognition.

Processing Speed

It refers to how easily information can be interpreted and then generated by the brain, such as making a gesture or delivering a response. Processing velocity affects just about every brain function. Processing speed is not a specific mental task in itself. It's about how easily you can handle a mental job. Rate of processing declines with age, with one expert defining it as an almost linear decline. The fall starts in early adulthood, so as long as people are in their 70's or 80's, processing speed is significantly lower compared to one's 20's age.

Memory

This is a broad category that covers the ability to recall information. Main subtypes include:

Working memory It refers to the ability to keep information in mind briefly and mentally manipulate it, including remembering a new phone number and then dialing it.

- Working memory includes a variety of mental functions, including problem-solving, decision-making, and language processing.

- Long-term semantic memory, it applies to the factual information you gain over time, such as the name of the state capital.

- Episodic memory. This applies to one's mind for specific observed events that have occurred at a given time or place.

- Prospective memory. This refers to the ability to remember going forward to do things.

- Procedural memory. This is also called capacity learning. This applies to study and reminding of how to do certain things.

- Building up usually requires time and practice.

Memory is also a complicated topic, many other subtypes can be described, and researchers are also still researching how to categorize and explain the many different ways that people remember knowledge or how to do stuff. Technically, generating a memory (which is sometimes called encoding) and recalling it is also a different task for the brain. So, a person may have issues in remembering something either because they were having trouble encoding it in the first place, or because they are having trouble getting it back promptly. Some memory aspects decline with age, but not all: memory types that reject: working memory episodic memory (especially for more recent events). Prospective memory types that stay stable Procedural memory Semantic long-term memory (may decline after the 7th decade).

Attention

Attention is the ability to focus and concentrate on something important to process-related information. Main subtypes include:

- Selective attention. This is the ability to focus on something particular despite the presence of other distracting knowledge or stimuli that are "irrelevant." Examples: finding the relevant information on a cluttered website while being in a busy environment, following a conversation.

- Divided focus, Also known as "multi-tasking," that is the ability to manage multiple tasks or information sources simultaneously. Examples: while listening to music, reading a recipe, driving while talking to someone.

- Sustained concentration. This is the ability to stay focused on something for an extended period.

With aging, some aspects of attention get worse. Specifically: With aging, selective attention gets worse. Foraging, the split focus gets worse. The sustained concern with aging doesn't seem to get worse.

Executive Functioning

It applies to the mental skills needed for planning, organizing, problem-solving, abstract thinking, mental flexibility, and effective behavioral behaviors. Executive function helps people to do things like: solve new problems. Organize information and schedule tasks. Think abstractly Using rationale (especially when it comes to explaining with unfamiliar material), adapt to new situations, behave in socially appropriate ways, make complex decisions how it changes with aging: Executive function generally decreases with age, especially after period 70.

Emotional Processing

This refers to how one expresses and regulates emotions, particularly that contrary. Factors include: How quickly one gets out of a negative emotional state, how physically or emotionally sensitive one is to interpersonal stressors, behavioral techniques to reduce negative stimuli, such as paying little attention to the How it improves with aging. Older adults undergo many changes that generally make them more positive and hopeful. These include: paying less attention to negatively simulating conditions or removing them. Paying more attention to anything good. Remembering positive things more.

Chapter 5: Parenting Role in Nurturing Child's Brain

The development of children's cognitive and social skills needed for later school success can best be facilitated by a parenting style known as sensitive parenting. Responsiveness is an aspect of positive parenting that is defined through various theories and research contexts (e.g., attachment, socio-cultural) as playing an essential role in providing children with a strong foundation for successful growth.

The effective-emotional aspects of a sensitive style are parenting that offers healthy affection and high levels of comfort, and is responsive in ways that are contingently linked to the signals of a young child ("contingent responsiveness").

Such factors, combined with activities that relate cognitively to the needs of the child, including providing precious verbal feedback and sustaining and enhancing the interests of the child, provide the continuum of support needed for multiple aspects of the learning of the child.

Acceptance of the child's attention with prompt and flexible responses to what the child communicates facilitates learning, in part, by encouraging the creation of the child's strategies for coping with stress and excitement in its environment. Through repeated positive experiences, the child and the parent build a confidence and connection that, in effect, helps the child to internalize this trust and then generalize their learning into new experiences.

Such proactive support facilitates the ongoing involvement of the child with his or her parent in learning activities.

Therefore, these affective-emotional behaviors reflect the parent's concern and approval, promoting self-regulation and co-operation, which are critically essential behaviors for active learning. From a socio-cultural point of view, cognitive sensitive activities (e.g. holding interests versus redirecting interests, rich verbal input) are thought to promote higher learning levels because they provide a foundation or scaffold for the immature skills of the young child, such as improving focus and cognitive abilities. In this context, sensitive actions encourage mutual participation and reciprocity within parent-child interaction, and help a child learn to play a more involved and eventually independent part in the learning process. Responsive encouragement for the child to actively engage in problem solving is often referred to as parental scaffolding, and is also believed to be crucial to promoting the development of children's self-regulation and executive function skills, behaviors that eventually allow the child to assume responsibility for their wellbeing.

5.1 Effect of Parenting on Development of Child's Brain

Responsive parenting is one of the most often discussed elements of parenting as we try to know the role that the environment plays in developing children.

Parenting strategies around the world share three main goals, according to the American Psychological Association: ensuring the health and safety of children, preparing children for life as productive adults, and communicating cultural values. Those targets are optimistic. Being a good parent is no small feat and depends on several environmental and biological factors on how children become capable, happy, productive adults.

There are various factors on child outcomes, but a wealth of literature suggests that parenting is an essential part of the equation. The degree to which parenting strategies influence behavioral development in children is a complex issue. While we may not be able to answer it with confidence, we can be sure that parents are essential factors in the behavioral outcomes of their children. Research shows that it can encourage appropriate developmental trajectories for children at high risk, such as those from low-income families and those with very premature births.

Research has found strong linkages between parenting and change of child behavior. For example, parenting practices of a mother, including the degree to which she shows affection towards and maintains behavioral and psychological influence over her child when that child is five years of age, is related to later internalizing and outsourcing behaviors of the child. Internalizing behavioral problems, or emotional ones, also relate to anxiety and depression. Externalizing, or destructive, behavioral problems are commonly associated with attention deficit hyperactivity disorder and conduct issues. These are just a few typical behavioral issues which are partially influenced by specific parenting styles. Unresponsive parenting, by contrast, can jeopardize the development of children, particularly those at higher risk for developmental problems.

 Recent evidence suggesting correlations between high levels of early responsive parenting and more significant hippocampal volumes for typically developing preschool-aged children highlights the critical importance of responsive parenting. Increased capacity in this brain region is associated with several psychosocial variables

(e.g., stress reactivity) progressing more optimally.

Links between early responsive parenting and increased volume in the hippocampal region also indicate that the first developmental period is an essential time for promoting responsive parenting practices, especially in high-risk families, to improve the relationship between parent and child. Given the potential value of proactive parenting, our awareness of how to promote successful parenting activities could be further enhanced by more specific knowledge of the types of behaviors most necessary to support specific areas of child learning.

The learning of problem-solving, vocabulary, and social-emotional skills by young children is encouraged by experiences with their parents. There is some evidence that in this parenting style, the mechanism by which responsively promotes the development of a child can rely on consistency through development. Since the child and the parent are part of a broader social context, many factors may support or impinge on the consistent use of responsive behaviors by a parent. Personal factors that may undermine the sensitivity of a parent include stress, the view of the parent's own experience of child-rearing as unfavorable, or beliefs and attitudes that distract from a parent's sense of importance in the life of his or her or her child. Other variables, however, such as higher levels of social support from friends and family, can mitigate some of these negative social-personal factors as well as predict which parents move with intervention from a non-responsive to a responsive style. This is a promising finding since parenting strategies can be designed to provide mothers from high-risk social backgrounds with a level of social support needed to develop sensitive parenting styles.

Responsive parenting is an essential process for supporting the learning of young children according to many descriptive studies and fewer experimental studies.

A causal role of responsive parenting is now recognized, as more significant improvements in parental behaviors associated with responsive style were responsible for the impact of multiple parenting interventions on more significant gains in learning for young children. Recent evidence for typically developing children showing linkages between early high levels of responsive parenting and increased volume in brain regions responsible for stress regulation also suggests the critical importance of rapid development of this parenting practice. Because both routine and high-risk children enjoyed responsiveness that offered affective-emotional and cognitively responsive support, the efficacy of responsiveness is best understood when identified as a specific construct. Recent evidence shows that certain reactive behaviors can provide different kinds of support for the learning of children, and this support may vary depending on the developmental needs of a child. Many new research directions need to be explored, and issues that need further review are discussed in recent studies.

The attempt to research the effect of parenting strategies on child outcomes is complicated because an incredibly wide range of parenting activities and an equally wide array of child behavioral outcomes occur.

The causal relationship between parenting practices and consequences of child behavior is similarly opaque, depending on the timing and measurement of the actions at issue. For example, in a study of adolescents' understanding of the psychological control of their parents,

or the degree to which parents attempt to control the emotions and beliefs of their children,

and the self-reported internalizing and violent behaviors of adolescents, researchers and scientists discovered behavior of a child as a powerful predictor of changes in parental psychological control than parental behavior as a predictor of changes. Because this connection is multi-directional, it becomes even more challenging to research the effect of parenting strategies on child behavioral outcomes.

5.2 Parenting Styles

A common way of dealing with these complexities is to organize parenting behaviors into four distinct parenting styles: authoritarian, permissive, implicated, and authoritative). These four parenting ways are based on two parental dimensions: parental warmth related to the child's parental affection and acceptance, and parental control related to the active role parents play in promoting compliance with rules and social conventions. Extensive research has been done on the implications of parenting styles on children's behavioral outcomes.

Authoritarian Parenting Style

The strict parent blends low warmth with high control levels and employs a rigid parenting style marked by minimal interaction with the infant, high expectations, restricted tolerance, constant use of punishment, and one-way parent-to-child contact. Authoritarian parenting was linked to child outcomes such as hostility, delinquency, rebelliousness, and anti-social aggression. Research has also found that early experience of an infant with excessive parental control appears to correlate with anxiety development. This fear is likely due to a lack of opportunity to develop autonomy through autonomous environmental exploration. It has also been recommended that the low warmth characteristic of authoritarian parenting may be associated with childhood depression.

Permissive Parenting Style

The permissive parent shows high warmth levels and low control levels. He or she behaves more like a friend than a parent, using a loose form of discipline with few guidelines, little to no standards, and little supervision or direction. Parents with this style tend to be very affectionate and caring, but also allow their children to solve problems without the intervention of the parents. Significant predictors of child behavior problems reported by both parents and teachers were in a permissive parenting survey, lack of participation, lack of follow-up, and lack of confidence in parenting. Because permissive parents tend to be non-demanding, control of the actions of children, and define limits in children's environments becomes much more difficult. Research has found correlations between the excessive parental indulgence often seen in permissive parenting activities and the reduced social skills and academic achievement of children. Permissive parenting has been associated with bossy, dependent, impulsive behavior in children with low self-control and achievement rates, and a failure to learn resilience and emotional control.

Uninvolved Parenting Style

The uninvolved parent combines low warmth and low control levels and uses no particular style of discipline. Sometimes, he or she shows no interest in being a mom. Communication is limited. Nursing is low, and, in general, the child has excessive freedom. Since the uninvolved parent is neither demanding nor attentive, and since the young children are highly dependent on parental structure and care, uninvolved parenting has been associated with behavioral problems and depression in children.

Furthermore, teenagers who are subject to uninvolved parental activities also experience high rates of alienation and appear to exhibit more externalizing attitudes, aggressive behaviors, criminal behaviors, aggression, and attention problems. The consequences of unchanged parenting may also extend through puberty and into adulthood. Researchers found in a study of first Year College students that individuals who reported being raised by uninvolved parents showed more internalizing and outsourcing issues in reaction to negative emotions such as homesickness. However, these students were significantly less successful in dealing with problems than individuals who described growing up in a loving home environment.

Authoritative Parenting Style

The dominant parent displays both high warmth levels and high control levels. People in this group are compassionate and caring, set high standards, clearly explain discipline guidelines, and communicate with their children in frequent communication.

Authoritative parenting has been linked to increased child competence, great maturity, assertiveness, and self-control. Authoritarian parents who use child-centered parenting methods and use verbal reasoning and explanations tend to raise children with high levels of moral reasoning, moral awareness markers, and prosaically behavior.

Evidence has shown that authoritarian parenting can be the most effective type, but in terms of parental energy and time, it also appears to be the most demanding. Parents living under adverse circumstances, such as deprivation, may be less likely to exhibit authoritarian parenting strategies and more likely to use less successful parenting practices.

Research suggests that parents with a higher socioeconomic status household are more likely to adopt egalitarian and child-centered parenting methods, as compared to the hierarchical and parent-centered style that characterizes homes with lower socioeconomic status. This would guide to an increased likelihood of raising children who show problems of internalizing and outsourcing behavior, which, in effect, is likely to place more burden on the family. The circular pattern has enormous implications for the future because it leads to structural inequity of deprivation for families.

Implications of Positive Parenting Style

Parents have to find a parenting style that works best for them and their kids. Authoritative and redirection have a positive effect on a child's cognitive development.

Hence the child has higher self-esteem and academic success. Authoritarian, forgiving. And uninvolved tend to affect the cognitive development of a child negatively.

Therefore, the child has lower self-esteem and less academic achievement. Parenting is successful when the parent is warm and caring, yet challenging, on the cognitive development of the child.

Parents should allow for independence and discovery, but they should set limits.

Observing their actions is critical for parents because it affects the cognitive development of a child. Whatever parenting methods are used, parents should aspire to use some sound principles to allow the child to develop independence, self-esteem, and maturity.

There are many policy implications for the value of sensitive parenting for the welfare of young children.

Policy and practice decision-makers need to pay particular attention to parents who are most at risk, to optimize performance, they need to find ways to promote improvement in parent behavior, taking into account factors such as parent values, social support, and mental health status. The synthesis of relevant research will direct new investment in parent services as well as the creation of proactive parenting research initiatives. Developmental science is often not well incorporated into the implementation of policies or programmers. Considering the critical role early experience plays in brain development, policymakers have an interest in ensuring that the atmosphere for young children (e.g., home, child care) is of sufficient quality to promote positive outcomes. As new investments are made in publicly funded child and family care, the focus on transparency is often higher. This should help to encourage more significant consideration of evidence-based research that can better guarantee the feasibility of the program.

5.3 Effects of Negative Parenting Style on Child's Brain

While parenting is not always sunshine and roses, concentrating too much on the thunderclouds could put your child in an inferior position. Parents have a strong influence on the actions of their children. Kids are like sponges — they model everything that a parent does and integrate into their own lives what they see. It's crucial that parents set their children the right examples. Negative examples may affect the growth of a child and may lead to bad behavior. Negative tactics of parenting, such as lecturing, moaning, threatening, and yes, even nagging, will seriously affect the actions and activities of your child later on in life. What does happen at home affect the long-term mental health and development of children? But it's not just the parent-child relationship, which is essential. The way parents get along also plays a significant role in the wellbeing of a child, which can affect everything from mental health to academic success and future relationships. Bad parenting is defined as a sequence of actions that can affect the personality and psychology of the child severely. Bad parenting is not confined to a single act; it is a collection of these acts that usually contribute to the child's harmful effect. Most poor parenting may not be deliberate, but this does not reduce the negative impact it has on the infant. Some parents are unaware of the consequences of these acts, and some may not even know. Poor parenting could be caused by not knowing enough to be a better parent or by a general lack of apathy to learn the right way. There exists no relationship that is entirely free of conflict and dispute, and indeed, all the children see their parents argue at some point. Parents relate calmly and positively to each other during a disagreement, solve the problem, and show the children through their subsequent interactions that the conflict has been resolved. The children may not be affected by conflict (few of the research suggests that they may even understand skills related to the resolution of disputes that they can apply to their relationships along the way). (The impact of observing domestic violence on children is not discussed in detail in this book, but it has also, of course, been shown to be very harmful). And conflict is damaging whether parents are married or even living together. The UK and international research conducted over several decades through home observations, long-term follow-up work, and experimental studies suggest that children exposed to conflict may have higher heart rates and reactions to stress hormones from as young as six months. As a result of living with extreme or prolonged inter-parental battle, babies, children, and adolescents may show signs of disturbed early brain development, sleep disturbance, anxiety, depression, conduct disorder, and other pressing issues.

From a very early age— some researchers say as young as six months— children show anxiety when their parents fight. Their reactions may include anger, fear, sadness, and anxiety, and there is an excessive possibility of experiencing a wide variety of problems related to health, disturbed sleep, and trouble concentrating and succeeding in school. They may "externalize" their distress in the form of "aggression, hostility, anti-social and non-compliant behavior, delinquency, and vandalism," or "internalize" it in the way of "depression, anxiety, withdrawal, and dysphoria." Moreover, "children in high-conflict homes are more likely to have poor interpersonal skills, problem-solving skills, and social skills."

Research Study on Negative behavior of Mothers towards Children

Researchers at the University of Minnesota researched more than 260 mothers and their kids from birth to first grade. Based on both findings and parent accounts, they assessed the complicated disposition of children as well as how they were looked after between the first week of their birth and the sixth month of life. When the kids were two and a half and three years old, the researchers looked at mothers with their kids doing tasks that challenged the kids and required parental assistance. Researchers defined negative parenting occurs when parents expressed their children's negative emotions, handled them roughly, and the like.

The researchers also found that it was an escalating or progressive conflict that predicted later conducting problems between moms and their infants–that is, a conflict that worsened over time.

And in a cyclical pattern, when moms were negatively parenting their infants, that resulted in their children showing high levels of anger as infants, which in turn caused more hostility from the moms. Besides, moms who had negative parenting of their infants may also have had angrier children because these moms were more hostile towards their infants. Negative parenting in infancy seemed to set the stage for both moms and their children to be more hostile and angrier in their childhood, bringing out the worst in each other. The results of our research go beyond descriptive findings to clarify the fundamental mechanism of connecting how mothers raise and look after their children in their childhood and children's issues in early primary education. Researchers suppose that the outcomes of the study can help in developing appropriate interventions for targeting negative parenting — starting as early as three months— to help prevent problems in children later on.

Chapter 6: Ways to Improve Baby's Brain Development

The way a child thinks acquires information and communicates with its surrounding environment is characterized by cognitive development. Different cognitive abilities are gained as a child reaches certain developmental milestones, but practices that encourage active learning will support a child of any knowledge. As a parent, by integrating basic tasks into your daily routine, you can facilitate your child's cognitive development in the areas of memory, focus, attention, and perception. The brain of an infant needs a stimulating environment where it can develop. Children fulfill their curiosities by their day-to-day tasks and explorations. Children have the most compelling interest in learning about the world. Families need to create a healthy, stimulating environment that allows children to develop their cognitive abilities. Since most kids learn through play, parents can use various games and toys to target particular mental recourses. Ultimately, that will provide your children with a fun experience and, at the same time, develop their cognitive domains. New parents want to make the best start in life for their infant, and a large part of encouraging early baby brain growth stimulates the brain of your baby. It may appear like an intimidating task, but it doesn't have to be challenging to improve your small mind.

6.1 Developing Cognitive Skills in Children

Provide a loving environment

Providing a nurturing environment is an essential factor in your children's cognitive development.

A concentrative atmosphere with both physical and verbal expressions of love will create the ideal atmosphere for developing the emotional skills of your child and for building a strong bond between you and your child. This boosts their self-confidence and allows them to focus their attention on other developmental aspects, as they don't have to waste time seeking approval and love. Children also get to know how to express affection through kisses, hugs, massages, and general touch and use body language as a means of communication successfully.

Exercise the Body

Exercise is essential to the development of the brain, and hence cognitive thinking. Children oxygenate the brain faster through use and physical activity, and that helps it develop. In turn, they create stronger synaptic connections through the growth of their motor skills, which help to respond to muscle nerve in a faster brain. Going outside allows for the absorption of fresh air and offers a healthy physical growth environment. Swimming, however, is the best exercise of all, as it includes all muscle groups.

A Good Sleep

Sleep helps the brain to refresh and process all of the information learned every day. A child needs 8 to 10 hours of good, high-quality sleep to recover and energize itself. Parents should make use of the time right before bedtime to reflect on the day's actual events and specific ways of demonstrating passion. This will develop a sense of well-being, resulting in optimistic visions that will ignite creativity and imagination.

Healthy Food for Fast Cognitive Functioning

Healthy brain growth demands a healthy diet. Parents should provide a varied and nutritious diet for their children that includes fresh produce, meat, and dairy products.

Protein-rich foods are essential to brain growth by helping the brain to absorb more mass. Omega-3 fats (usually come up with fish, nuts, and eggs) also help in concentration, acquisition of knowledge, and logical thinking. Therefore, adding them into your child's diet will aid in their cognitive development.

Learning through Fun

By play, children learn most about the world around them. In some areas of cognitive development, almost all behaviors can benefit. Parents can provide different toys for their children and teach different games for children to target specific cognitive development. This can include the event of any type of skills: from language, concentration, creativity, logical and abstract thinking, to physical abilities such as hand-eye coordination, individual awareness, and motor functions.

Singing them a Song

Let's be honest: while you're in the front seat focusing on the road, there's not too much you can do with your baby, and your baby stares at the upholstery on the back of the rear seat. But singing is a hands-free activity, and it will significantly boost the development of his baby's brain. When parents sing to babies, they often sing with a lot of intonation, which is of interest to the baby. "Songs can familiarize with new words and repetitive patterns which are essential to the development of language. Singing often teaches babies about rhyming, which is vital for later reading success.

Take Child to Grocery Shopping

You may be tempted to keep your baby occupied with a phone or tablet when you have your baby in the cart. "Describe the places, the odors, the shapes.

Let the baby hold a kiwi and show him how different it feels from an orange." You can also call out colors and count fruit and vegetables as you place them in a jar. And your babe will love a "Where did it go!" game. You plop items in the cart behind him (and you're going to love that he's learning object permanence).

Taking to Walk

There's so much your baby needs to see when you're out for a stroll, says Shaw. Point things like the stars, trees, and birds and call them, and improve the growth of the baby's brain by using words to describe the rhythm of different terrain you're walking over: "This path is bumpy" and "The road is smooth." If your walker moves so that your baby faces you, she'll be able to watch your mouth while you're forming sentences, which will help her learn to speak.

Mealtime In a high chair

Babies play a universal game; let me drop this food (or spoon, or cup, or toy) on the floor and see what's going on! But it is not just fun— it's another opportunity to learn the permanence of things. She is also working on her hold as she picks up foods with small fingers, an essential skill in fine motors. Mealtime can also be used to teach your baby new concepts, such as different textures, and to describe the difference between hot and cold.

Bedtime

Most parents include a bedtime story as part of the end-of-day routine that's a great way to boost the growth of the baby brain.

"Make time to read or just look at pictures in a book, right from birth.

"You don't have to read a story from start to finish." The bedtime routine is also a wonderful time of bonding. "We know that the way they learn is when babies and children have a secure attachment. Then they fall asleep, and the brain becomes refreshed for another day of development and discovery.

6.2 Improving Cognitive skills through Games

Cognitive development means the way kids think, learn, and find out things. It is the creation of awareness, skills, and strategies that help children think about the world around them and appreciate it. Fostering the cognitive development of your child as soon as he/she is born provides the basis for both school and later life success. Here are suggestions for promoting cognitive development through various activities.

Memory games help to build short- and long-term memory. Besides that, they have practical implications since they can enhance all three forms of learning (visual, auditory, and kinesthetic). Challenges of verbal and picture recall, puzzles, and pantomimes all help improve memory skills.

Word and number games like Sudoku games and crossword puzzles help improve the logical thinking, pattern recognition, and language skills of your child.

Simple games also provide a way for child to expand his or her vocabulary and adjust to a symbolic way of thinking. Sudoku and crosswords also have health benefits, because they minimize the likelihood of dementia and Alzheimer's. Reading is another activity which makes cognitive development better.

Kids can improve their imagination and visualization skills through stories. In fact, the reading process itself lets them learn vocabulary and develop their linguistic competencies.

Parents must provide age-appropriate books to their children. Their first collection of books should have plenty of colors and illustrations to attract attention and spark interest so that your child will want to pick up books themselves later on. Reading books also features top watching films, as they are more engaging and require more mental recourse.

Performance is another way to help children develop cognitive competencies. Music listening is a great stress reduction tool, and it provides a healthy and toxic-free atmosphere where the brain can grow properly. Playing musical instruments is a way of developing coordination and creativity, which stimulates emotion. The drums, keyboards, and piano are the most engaging instruments for children because they produce both hemispheres of the brain in an identical comparison, through coordinated use.

Today's technological advances have provided children with several ways to develop their cognitive abilities, primarily through child-friendly computer games. Online math and word games are interactive learning sources allowing parents also to participate. And, as most of them are time-based, they develop rapid thinking, quick memory retrieval, and improved decision-making and speed of reaction.

6.3 Cognitive Nurturing in Early Childhood

Parents should facilitate practices that will enhance the mental development of young children. Pre-operative children (age 2 to 7 years) learn efficiently, so direct play and interaction are the best vehicles to teach them concepts. There are a lot of fun practical skills that children can learn to improve their focus, memory, abstract thinking, and ability to make decisions. Age-appropriate puzzles are fun challenges that promote skills in problem-solving and critical thinking. Easy board games can also develop problem-solving skills and teach young kids how to follow a set of instructions.

Additionally, games and puzzles can help teach categorization (e.g., sorting by type, shape, or color), concentration, and memory skills into groups. The rules and aims of the games they play can become more complicated and exciting as children grow. Classic games such as checkers are useful to introduce right now. There are plenty of fun puzzles and board games to buy in the store, but families can easily make their own too. Extra photos or large magazine pictures, for example, can be covered with bright plastic contact paper, and then cut into big inconsistent, irregular shapes to create puzzles.

Young children continue to take advantage from make-believe play throughout the pre-operative period. Children learn to stretch out their imagination and creative thinking skills by creating their imaginary setting and placing themselves within it. Most kids spontaneously play "pretend" games in which they act as something other than themselves, a dinosaur or a princess. Though parents may not find such games meaningful, children will still generally benefit from playing them. By merely jumping into the game as best they can, parents will promote such make-believe games. Most children will be gleefully playing along with mom or dad. Many kids, however, have an internalized collection of instructions or values that surround their make-believe scene and will immediately correct any adult who doesn't abide by those arcane rules that seem so clear to them. As long as kids don't hit or scream to make a point, parents should just play along and adjust as best they can to the creative thinking train of their child.

When children are themselves out of ideas, parents can take a turn creating the setting to make-believe and encourage the little ones to play along.

The make-believing play of parents can be as dumb and off-the-wall as the result of their kids, or it can be more organized to provide lessons on specific topics. Maintaining and loving scenes (such as taking care of a baby or playing house) or rough and tumble, immersive scenes (such as playing good guys versus bad guys or pretending to be a wild animal) can include themes for adult-driven make-believe play. Parents should promote a variety of different playing types (even if they aren't always excited about playing all kinds themselves). As long as play themes aren't hurtful or violent, they're probably okay.

May be improved by using props or masks to make-believe "pretend" games. Parents should buy all sorts of dress-up clothes and plastic toys that mimic adult items (such as kitchens, vehicles, lightsabers, etc.). Make-believe props needn't be expensive, though. An old Mom's shirt plus pieces of ribbon that serves as a gown for the ball. Hats from the old trunk of clothing that Grandma has can work well as accessories. The kitchen table with a table cloth spread over the top can also become a cave, while a couple of empty toilet paper rolls taped together and decorated can become the wand of a magician. Creating the rod or other props may turn into a craft project.

Because kids of this age learn so much through making-believe play, it's no surprise that many young kids like to pretend they do whatever activities they see their parents do around the house.

Families can exploit the natural interest of children in adult activities by enlisting them to help with household chores. Although chore operation can seem monotonous to adults,

it can serve as educational opportunities for children. For example, younger kids can sort laundry into various piles based on the type of color and clothing (e.g., pants vs. shirts).

Older preschoolers can help to make meals or snacks, an activity that can teach them how to make healthy food choices, safety in the kitchen, and the art of making tasty foods. Young children of school age can be given routine tasks to complete and take pride in, such as setting the dining table, making their beds, or putting away their clothes. The creation of recipes can be a fun activity for all ages. When children are helping with chores and household tasks, it is essential to remember that the description of "help" may require to be made quite flexible, especially when very young children are "helping." Some of what kids think help will be detrimental from the adult perspective. Parents should remain calm and encouraging to help children, wherever possible, rather than toughly correct them for failing to meet adult standards. Waiting until the child is distracted or otherwise occupied is best before taking over and correcting any mistakes that children may have made. The point of letting children to help with household chores and events is to encourage family bonding, and to boost learning opportunities and self-esteem for children, not to perfect the household cleaning program.

Chapter 7: Impact of External Surrounding on Brain Development

Several research studies have shown in recent years that early-life experiences can influence brain development in children. Two recently published studies have further clarified early-life influences on brain growth and behavior. Joan Luby and colleagues reported in an article published in the Proceedings of the National Academy of Sciences USA (PNAS) that increased parental support during pre-school years is associated with faster growth of the brain's hippocampal region as quantifying by neuroimaging. Those children with great motherly support had a double increase in this region's growth rate as compared with children with lower maternal support levels. The research team also showed that higher growth rates in hippocampal areas were interlinked with better emotional growth.

In a different study published in Biological Psychiatry, Scott Mackey and colleagues studied the correlation between childhood adversity, impulsivity, brain growth patterns, and antisocial behavioral development. They found that higher impulsivity levels were associated with lower growth in specific neocortex regions, and increased growth in specific subcortical brain regions.

Childhood adversity influenced the growth patterns in brain regions thought to contribute to impulsivity, and these growth patterns were associated with antisocial behavior development.

These two studies strongly recommend that environmental influences on young children have direct effects on brain maturation patterns, which, in turn, are linked to specific behavior patterns.

Others will increasingly employ the approaches used by these investigators to determine the roles of psychosocial influences in children and adolescents on regional brain development. Such data will enhance our understanding of neurodevelopment relationships, the environment, brain structures, and specific behaviors, including psychiatric diseases. Elucidating structural changes associated with environmental challenges and improved methods for quantifying ecological variables can also provide measurable markers that would help to determine the effectiveness of early interventions. For example, would the degree of hippocampal growth have associated with better emotional development in adolescents and young adults in response to therapies aimed at improving parental support? Would the degree of normalization of cortical and subcortical growth patterns through specific therapies targeting impulsive behaviors minimize the development of antisocial behaviors? Neuroimaging methods provide more sophisticated tools critical to advancing our understanding of normal and abnormal brain development ever. Therefore, these approaches may be useful in predicting risks for the development of different psychological conditions and in assessing the effect of psychiatric illness prevention interventions on children at high risk.

7.1 Early Childhood Experiences Effect Brain for Long Term

For a lifetime, what happens in early childhood can be significant. To manage the future of our society successfully, we need to recognize and address problems before they get worse.

Work on stress biology in early childhood demonstrates how severe trauma, such as extreme poverty, violence, or neglect, can disrupt the production of brain architecture and permanently high-alert the body's stress response system. Science also suggests that providing stable, responsive, nurturing relationships in the earliest years of life can prevent or even reverse the harmful effects of early-life stress, with lifelong learning, behavior, and health benefits. It is long known that experiences of early childhood can have a profound impact on later chances and life opportunities. Now, a collection of new studies recommend that those experiences can affect the brain's size and function. Children are born ready to learn, and over many years, they have many skills to learn. As their first teachers, they rely on parents, family members, and other cares to build the right talent to become independent and lead healthy and prosperous lives. The way the brain develops is strongly affected by the interactions the child has with other people and the world. Nursing the mind is critical for the growth of the brain. In a safe environment where they are protected from neglect and extreme or chronic stress, the children grow and learn best. External with plenty to play and explore. Through talking to, playing with, and caring for their infant, parents and other cares will encourage healthy brain development. Children learn best when parents speak and play turns, and build on the skills and interests of their children. Nursing a child by knowing their needs and sensitively reacting to them helps protect the brains of children against stress. Speaking with kids and exposing them to books, stories, and songs help to strengthen the language and communication of children, which puts them on a path to learning and success in school. Stress and stress exposure can have long-term detrimental effects on the brain of the infant while speaking, reading, and playing can promote brain growth. It is a critical public health priority to make sure that parents, caregivers, and early childhood care providers have the tools and expertise to provide healthy, secure, caring, and stimulating care. If children are at risk, monitoring the development of children and ensuring they meet developmental milestones will help ensure early detection of any issues, and children may obtain the support they may need.

The brain undergoes it most fastly growth from the fetal era through the first years of life, and early experiences decide whether its construction is robust or fragile. The circuitry of the brain is most open to the influence of external expertise, for better or for worse, during the early sensitive periods of development. Healthy emotional and cognitive development during these

vulnerable times is influenced by receptive, dependable contact with adults, whereas persistent or extreme adversity can disrupt healthy brain development.

For example, children who were placed in orphanages shortly after birth with conditions of severe neglect show dramatically reduced brain activity compared with children who have never been institutionalized.

Understanding how to deal with challenges is a vital part of having healthy children.

Our bodies cause several physiological responses when we're threatened, including changes in heart rate, blood pressure, and stress hormones like cortisol.

When a young child is supported by nurturing relationships with adults, he learns to cope with daily challenges and returns to normal with his stress response system. Scientists refer to that as positive stress.

Tolerable stress occurs when more severe difficulties, such as a loved one's loss, a natural disaster, or an alarming injury, are buffered by caring adults who help the child adapt, mitigating the potentially harmful effects of abnormal stress hormone levels. Without adult intervention, stress is toxic when massive, regular, or sustained adverse experiences such as extreme poverty or persistent violence are encountered, as excessive cortisol interferes with the production of brain circuits. Toxic stress encountered early in life and familiar precipitants of toxic stress — such as poverty, abuse or neglect, abuse of parental substances or mental illness, and exposure to violence — can affect a person's physical and psychological health cumulatively. The more painful and damaging childhood experiences, the higher and more significant the likelihood of developmental delays, and other issues. Adults with more negative early childhood experiences are also more likely to experience health issues, including obesity, depression, heart disease, and diabetes.

7.2Environmental Impact on Child's Brain Development

Human beings have had to be sensitive to their surroundings since the earliest times to survive, which means we have an innate awareness of our surroundings and are looking for environments with certain qualities. First of all, humans have a deep need for safety and security and look in their surroundings for those attributes. We're also looking for physical comforts, like a proper temperature environment.

Furthermore, we're searching for a mentally comfortable environment: for example, familiar surroundings, while providing the right amount of stimulus.

Nature, as compared to nurture, is a topic of the great debate that has been undergoing on for many years, with people on both sides of the trouble agreeing that both genetics and environment play a significant role in a person's growth.

There is no question that both sides of these points are valid, especially when it comes to brain development and learning in children. While genetics are factor when it comes to the pruning of brain and the reorganization of the brain structure, the setting in which a child is exposed during the early years when brain development is at its peak has an immense influence on the development of his brain. To further understand this, below is a look at various environmental factors and how they might impact a child's brain growth.

Stimulants

Stimulants are one of the significant environmental factors affecting the development of a child's brain and his / her ability to learn and understand. During the early years of childhood, when brain growth and development are at their height, the mind of a child should be continuously stimulated using audio and visual stimulants to activate synaptic changes and reconstruction of neural pathways that characterize brain growth. The audio and visual stimulants that are the source of these alterations are found in the environment of the child and include music, sound patterns, speech, pictures, decorations, displays, etc. These audio and visual stimulants have a significant impact on the development of their brain. Depriving an infant of sight, for example, can cause the neural pathways involved insight to develop improperly, leading to problems like congenital cataracts. While on the other hand, a child who is disclosed to various visual stimulants can create a sharp perception of the environment, which helps him/her to interact with the environment easily and to recognize and identify different objects quickly. In the case of auditory stimulants, the situation is also similar where an infant can learn to speak and understand speech more rapidly if they are regularly spoken to and exposed to other sounds.

Drugs, contaminants, and diseases

Another significant environmental determinant that can have a substantial impact on a child's brain development is drugs, viruses, and toxins. Children who are open to (even before birth) to substances such as alcohol, nicotine (tobacco), and medications such as heroin and cocaine are at very high risk of slow brain development, leading to problems such as speech impairment, reduced mental abilities, poor language skills, low intelligence, and learning issues. Children who are open to numerous toxins such as lead, mercury, manganese, toxic solvents and other toxins found in their environment also face a high risk of developing cognitive problems such as poor memory formation, mental retardation, speech problems, hyperactivity, reduced IQ and poor motor skills. The case is also the same for children exposed to disease as different viruses and bacteria can have an important impact on the development of the brain by either hindering or lowering the rate of growth, thus affecting the ability of a child to learn and understand.

Abuse and neglect

Abuse and neglect are part of a child's emotional environment and have been shown to have a very significant negative impact on the child's brain development and learning skills. According to several studies, due to the constant state of fear and insecurity in which these children live, physical abuse, emotional abuse, and neglect of children during their early childhood years has a devastating impact on their brain development. As a result, they are at a high risk of having mental, behavioral, social, physical, and academic issues during their childhood and even adulthood years.

Love and emotional attachment

Love and emotional support from the other part of the loving environment to which a child may be exposed, and it also has a significant impact on the development of his or her brain. As seen from the abuse and neglect factor, the mind of a child is heavily influenced by the early-age emotional environment to which they are exposed. Unlike abuse and neglect, however, love and emotional support offer a positive influence by providing the children confidence and security and allowing them to develop a positive, loving environment. As a result, the brain develops quickly, healthily, flexibly, and in a variety of ways, and the child can obtain optimal cognitive functions. A loved child also acquires self-confidence, high self-esteem, and excellent social skills, and is thus capable of forming meaningful life relationships.

7.3 Brain Development Affected By Poverty

The stress of living in poverty affects the brains of children in ways similar to the effects of abuse. Many neglected children show high levels of stress, but there are an increase and decrease, said of the professor of psychology at the University of Wisconsin-Madison named Seth Polla. Poverty children may not reach those high levels of stress, but there is constant stress that never comes down. Pollak spoke about poverty neurobiology as part of the Sulzberger Distinguished Lecture Series presented by the Duke Center for Child and Family Policy. He and his colleagues looked at 823 brain scans of 431 children between the ages of 4 and 17 and lived in urban and rural areas. They found poverty affecting brain growth, and they can see the difference as early as infancy.

Children living in poverty have shown a different developmental trajectory as soon as age 2, recommending that the longer the child is open to an impoverished environment, the more significant the difference in brain development.

Also, the brain images of children living in poverty showed unusually high levels of cortisol — similar to those of children who were abused. That leads Pollak to believe the common denominator could be the stressful circumstances. The human brain is very adaptive, and human species are resilient. Poor children have a low level of approach to medical care, more exposure to toxins, more violence, and less inequality in income. If kids were only dealing with one thing, such as inadequate medical care, we would not see an effect. It's more than anyone can deal with having to deal with all of those factors. It is stressful, which ultimately inhibits developmental progress. Pollak said that the differences in brain growth and development could also impair educational achievement and executive function. A delay in the growth of the brain area that regulates problem-solving, attention, and judgment accounted for an achievement gap of 16 percent for high school students living below the federal poverty line. Similarly, a delay in the growth of the brain area, monitoring memory, emotion, and language accounted for a difference in the academic achievement of 21 percent. Consuming neuroscience to know that poverty is a relatively new method of research, and Pollak believes that this type of analysis can provide clues to targeting and refine youth interventions. No one likes child poverty-related outcomes. This scientific research indicates that poverty is not only a question of social policy but also of biomedicine.

7.4 Development Affected by Technology

Since media expansion to newer platforms, including cellphones and tablets, improved portability and connectivity has expanded the use of technology–not only for business professionals but for children. While television time is still the critical channel for children, clocking in at more than four hours per day on average.

According to a recent research study by the American Academy of Pediatrics, almost a third of the time is spent on a monitor, laptop, cell phone, and not in front of the television. What is also interesting is that mobile phones and tablets cannot be borrowed from a relative, considering that cell phone ownership among 12-to 17-year-olds has increased over the past decade, rising to an estimated 75 percent in 2004 to 45 percent of teenagers with their cell phones. Apart from watching television shows, preteens and adolescents most often use text to access social media. The question isn't whether children are increasingly exposed to technology–that's obvious–but what that exposure to technology means for childhood development. Many schools doll out smartphones for classroom events, while others are dolling out a fully technology-free environment. Although there have been influential voices in childhood development both for and against technology, it is essential to note that the impact of technology on childhood development may be more complicated than merely a "positive" or a "poor" phenomenon. Instead, we can collectively enhance the positive and work to reduce the negative by better understanding the overall effect.

Effects of Technology on Child Development

Harms Attention Spans

Perhaps the most frequently raised concern regarding children and technology is the impact on the span of attention. Research is backing this concern. In Psychology Today,

Jim Taylor, Ph.D., wrote that increased technology use could change the way children's brains are wired. Why? For what? Because unlike the mind of an adult, the spirit of a child still develops, and as a result, is malleable.

. When children are exposed to high-rates of technology, their brains may adopt an internet approach to thinking–quickly scanning and processing multiple information sources.

Brain development is particularly vulnerable to this, and where previous generations may have spent much more time reading, imagining, or participating in activities requiring focus attention. Brains in children open to the high intensity of technology may adapt to frequent visual stimulation, rapid change, and little need for imagination.

Reduces Self-Soothing and Self-Regulation

Anyone who has raised an infant would recognize the beauty of distraction in soothing an infant in a tantrum. But parents today are always given an enticing entertainment: technology. And while a screaming preschooler may be soothing in the immediate handing over of a cellphone or laptop, the American Academy of Pediatrics notes that the intrusion of mobile devices may negatively affect the ability for children to learn how to soothe themselves and control in those moments.

Increases Aggression

Multiple studies, including one conducted by the Seattle Children's Research Institute and the Youth and Adolescence Journal, found a correlation between simulated violence, often found in popular video games, and increased aggression. Exposure to violence has been found to make kids and teenagers more likely to argue with peers or teachers, and less empathic and impacted by actual violence.

Physical Activity Stagnates

The time that is spent on technology means time spent sitting. Even with portable devices, the operation itself demands that users remain mostly still. Given the vast amount of time that children are reportedly spending with technology now, this also means that this sedentary activity has now primarily replaced active indoor or outdoor playtime. In extreme cases, when engaged in a video game or other media, children or teenagers may even forgo other fundamental activities, likely eating or sleeping.

Hurts School Performance

Short periods of concentration can also affect how children take participate in the classroom. One experienced English teacher talked to the New York Times that because of cellphones and social media, students deprive of the attention span to read assignments alone. By watching YouTube, Facebook, Snapchat, texting, and e-mailing a bunch of abbreviations, you can't become a good writer. Technology habits the brains to continuously move between tasks, which may result in reduced spans of attention. Michael Rich, executive director of the Center for Media and Child Health in Boston, says that children's brains are rewarded for jumping to the next task rather than staying on the job, leading to "a generation of children in front of screens whose brains will be wired differently." Anecdotally, some teens admit that they prefer the immediate gratification provided by a quick video. Other scientific research recommends the availability of a computer can simply serve as a diversion, even if intended for educational purposes. In reality, Jacob L. Vigdor, an economics professor and researcher at Duke University, found that children most often used home computers for amusement rather than learning when left to themselves. Adult oversight is critical.

Limits Interpersonal interactions

Leaning to distract children on a mobile device can reduce their interpersonal interactions.

Whether it's a need to reconcile with a friend or sibling, have fun on a long trip, or settle down at night,

if children are always armed with technology, they're never going to navigate an interconnection with a friend, parent or sibling that may be critical to solving the problem in the long run.

Technology may act as a distraction from problematic issues for older children and teens: not fitting in at school, parents fighting at home, etc. But rather than learning to navigate these issues, children and teens may find that technology can give shelter illusion–without arming them with the interpersonal skills needed to navigate uncomfortable adult life situations.

Effects of Emotional Development

Even in the hands of only parents and careers, technology can have an impact on the development of childhood. Observation is the primary way children learn by listening to language learning, observing conversations, interpreting facial expressions, and watching how others handle emotional situations. Rampant screen time intentionally fades away, time connected with children that is critical to emotional development. A large dependency on technology to communicate hinders their people's skills for older children and teens and may even establish a sense of indifference from the feelings of others, according to the head of UCLA's memory and aging research Centre named Dr. Gary Small. The impact can be felt for young children as screen time replaces time previously devoted to playing, peer interaction, and exploration, which are thought to foster empathy, problem-solving skills, curiosity, intelligence, and listening skills, says Harvard-affiliated clinical psychologist Catherine Steiner-Adair. Boston University researchers also argue that the use of the mobile phone may prevent children from developing empathy, social skills, and problem-solving skills.

Visual-Spatial Helps

In fact, according to Science Daily, video games have been proven to help improve peripheral visual skills. More generally, with the use of technology, the general visual-motor skills (tracking objects or visually looking for something) can develop.

Helps Multi-Task

When appropriately implemented (as compared, for example, to driving and texting), a well-honed multi-task capacity brought about by the use of technology equips children with the abilities required for modern adult life, according to Psych Central.

Aids Learning

Internet users more frequently flex their brain decision-making and problem-solving functions and are more likely to handle quick cyber searches well. And, technology can present the next wave of vocational training for students who might not thrive on traditional academic subjects. The New York Times, for example, tells the story of Woodside High's audio class, filled with at-risk students engaged, engaged, involved, and learning. Not only is the technology-driven level inspiring students to show up, it provides job learning, and offers an opportunity to trigger interest in other topics. Besides, technology can support education in more traditional ways, including games to improve vocabulary, or through electronic books. Like with almost everything in existence, when implemented in moderation, technology is not a concern. Nonetheless, the numbers suggest that most have not yet reached the right healthy balance, as published rates are well above the standards of the American Academy of Pediatrics for electronic media. Given that the AAP recommends no access before age 2, and a limited 1-2 hours per day with entertainment media, it's secure to say that most kids surpass the limits suggested. We require to pursue a technology balance for our children, capitalize on the benefits, and mitigate the adverse effects of technology in the development of childhood.

7.5 Play deprivation can damage the childhood development of the brain

Individuals have similarities with extreme play-deprivation–especially young children who find themselves unable to play because, for example, they are caught up in conflicts, severe poverty, or abusive home environments. When these children do not play regularly, they may have real difficulty engaging with and healing from their encounters with the human community. That is because it is a sophisticated social and emotional learning experience that belongs to your social group, catalyzed by play. When they reach elementary school, children who are severely play-deprived may not have learned the complicated languages of the game that harmoniously combine the cognitive, emotional, physical, and social elements that are all necessary for personal skill in playing. Slowly occurs the social and emotional learning that allows for safe play among children.

A child who has not experienced good game early may overdo the process of playing, or may simply not know what is going on. These kids may get isolated or bullied, or they may become bullies. In later adult attitudes, the lingering effects of childhood play deficits echo about becoming a viable part of a community. Studies of rats reinforce the behavioral evidence around play-deprived children.

These experiments demonstrate the anatomical advantages of good play, which activates a wide range of genes in the prefrontal cortex.

This is the brain's executive area, which regulates rat decision-making as well as other social mammals, including humans. At Northwestern University, Jeffrey Burgdorf developed an experiment in which rats, aged between four and fifteen weeks, are engaged in rough and tumble play.

He discovered that between 300 and 1,200 genes had been activated in the prefrontal cortex after they had experienced the intense game. The late Jaak Panksepp, a play neuroscientist and co-author with Lucy Biven of' The Archaeology of the Mind,' proposed that play may trigger as many as 3,000 genes in the cortex. In short, play in the shaping of social brains seems essential. Rats don't work well if they don't play. They cannot make a distinction between friends and foes. They are not matting well, and in their responses to stress, they are less resilient than normal rats. "This work requires a more exceptional analysis. We still don't fully know the processes that release chemicals such as dopamine, endocannabinoids, opiates, and IGF-1 into the brain. Children who are severely play-deprived will tend to engage in automatic and repetitive activities without social involvement. A child who is deprived of play may have more explosive reactions to circumstances in later childhood, rather than a sense of belonging. They are often unoptimistic as adults and are subject to smoldering depression due to a lack of joy in their lives. We seem to be more politically set and confident in their social environments with little uncertainty. That's because playing promotes social and emotional learning and acceptance that ambiguity is part of complex interactions with people.

Chapter 8: Importance of Nurturing Child's Mind

What a person learns during childhood or does not learn will influence his future abilities. What, then, is it that children need from their parents to become balanced, successful adults? Remember what some have found in recent decades, based on research undertaken. Advances in brain imaging technology enable scientists to study the development of the brain more in-depth than ever before. These studies indicate that early childhood is a crucial time to develop the brain functions that are required to handle information, express emotions normally, and become language proficient. "In the early year's brain connections are wired at an extremely rapid rate, as the brain landscape is formed by moment-to-moment experiences of genetic information and environmental stimuli. Scientists believe that most of those associations are made in the first few years of life, called synapses. According to Dr. T. Berry Brazelton, a child development specialist,

this is when "the potential future wiring of a baby for intelligence, sense of self, confidence, and enthusiasm for learning is set."

During the initial few years, a baby's brain is growing dramatically in size, structure, and function. Synaptic links multiply in an environment that is rich in stimuli and learning experiences, producing a large network of neural pathways within the brain. Such pathways make it possible to think, understand, and reason. It may be that the more reproduction an infant's brain gets, the more nerve cells are turned on, and the more associations between them are made.

This stimulation is interestingly not merely intellectual, acquired through exposure to facts, figures, or language. Scientists have found the need for emotional enhancement, too. Research suggests that infants who are not held and touched and who are not being played or stimulated will develop less of these synaptic ties.

8.1 Children Develop Cynicism at Early Stage

Kids might not be as gullible as we would imagine. A new study shows the roots of cynicism are appearing as early as an elementary school in adolescents. Studies found that children are already suspicious of the things people tell them that they are in their self-interest by the time they're in second grade. As adults, we understand that the self-interests of an individual, such as their desire to gain attention or fit in with their peers, may affect what they say and believe about the world, "says a researcher from a psychology graduate student at Yale University, Candice Mills, in a press release. Our research study shows that children may be more naive, innocent, and trusting than adults, but there are also seeds of doubt in an ear. In the report, which appears in the current issue of Psychological Science, researchers examined what age children are beginning to take a cynical view of what people are saying to them. Researchers included twenty children each in kindergarten, second grade, and fourth grade, and told them short stories in which the characters made statements in or against their interests.

They found kids in kindergarten more likely to believe claims of self-interest in character. But by second-grade kids were already more critical and recognized that statements made in someone's self-interest might not be right. We question individuals who make statements in compliance with self-interest while growing their confidence in individuals who make statements against self-interest.

Researchers in the second part of the study asked the children which of three factors could cause somebody to make a false statement: deliberate deceit (lying), unintentional bias, or a simple mistake. Children of younger ages were more likely to think that lying was the best explanation for self-interest claims, whereas, in terms of being a mistake, they clarified incorrect statements against self-interest. Bias, as a possible explanation, was rarely supported by kindergarteners through fourth graders. Nevertheless, sixth-graders acknowledged both bias and lies as possible factors behind false statements made in an individual's self-interest. The authors write in this task that in a way, young children tend to be even more cynical than adults, assuming that people will intentionally mislead others even when they are not. There can be many causes for a cynic or pessimistic outlook, and symptoms of depression or anxiety can appear alongside them. For the latter, it may be a kind of defense mechanism to be cynic about a method or situation, a way to plan for the worst. And that can be both efficient and productive in some cases. From an evolutionary psychological perspective, most likely to succeed were our ancient predecessors, who always planned for the worst. The worst in those days was a predator attack, and the risk was serious damage or death. But the consequences are much less serious for our children today, and so that strategy serves little to no purpose. And start talking to your kids, and try to find out why they are and pessimistic and where they come from.

The first step is to try and understand where that cynicism could come from. There are many feasible causes. You know your child's attitude and behavior than anyone else and are likely in the leading and finest position to influence which of the following profiles most accurately describes his or her situation.

A cynic attitude may sometimes be embedded in the natural inborn temperament of a child.

Many children are easy-going; others are having difficulty adapting to transition. Some are aggressive and dominant, while others tend to be quieter and introvert.

Similarly, some kids have a naturally sunny disposition, while others are inclined to focus on life's wild side. The first group considers the glass half full, and the second half empty. Some studies indicate that those temperamental variations have an active genetic component. This is a consideration that you'll want to carefully consider when trying to get a handle on the attitude and behavior of your family. Hippocratic medicine and medieval psychology's four "touches of humor"-choleric (dominant, passionate, idealistic), confident -while not strictly "scientific" in the modern sense, may provide useful categories for thinking about distinctive personality types Your son may simply have a classic temperament for melancholy. But while character and biology can play an essential role in such a situation, environmental influences can be responsible as well.

To put it another way, children can learn that the people around them are negative. If mum and dad are serious about addressing this issue, they should start by questioning themselves some fair things. Could it be that they have restructured this kind of behavior and attitude towards their children? If you don't see yourself pessimistic now, might either you or your spouse have been discouraged or going through a particularly low point of life when your son was a baby and a mother? If not, could it be that you have made the mistake of reinforcing his anger by giving in and coddling his complaints? Perhaps your child did this in his early and younger age and see the effects only now.

Whether the issue is temperamental or environmental, you can fix it by making some changes to the style and methods of your parenting. Work on removing your child's moaning habit by avoiding him when he is negative. Don't give up on his dull mood.

When he begins to sob and moan about something, don't shower him with praise. When he talks about his day at school, or the birthday party he missed, or some activity he's just been involved in, tell him you're sorry he feels like that and then go about your business. Don't prolong debate. Only going on. While on the other hand, when your son says something encouraging or displays the slightest bit of excitement, you can reinforce the action by smiling, thanking him and letting him know how much you appreciate his upbeat attitude. You could even start rewarding him for positive statements and behavior by putting a star diagram on the fridge door and adding a sticker whenever he says or does something that brightens your day. That said, you should probably consider another possibility. There is a possibility that the negative attitude of your son might be clarified in terms of both factors including physical ones and biological ones. There is a psychiatric situation termed as dysthymia, which is in reality a low-grade depression of a long-term type. It is often characterized by a low level of energy, a lack of interest in life and even a recurrent pessimistic outlook.

8.2 Impact of Cynicism on Child's Life

Cynicism is part of a defensive stance we take to guard ourselves. It's typically triggered when children feel hurt or angry at something, and they allow them to fester and skew our outlook instead of addressing those emotions directly.

As child become pessimistic in their lives about one thing, they can slowly start turning everything on. When they become cynical, they often indulge in self-righteous attitudes and form expectations that individuals should behave in a certain way. Many of child's pessimistic emotions come up when they feel vulnerable.

Children are far more likely to react by toughening up and becoming aggressive at times when they feel helpless and are let down. Greater vulnerability to cynicism can be a sure sign they have turned themselves on. When they get into that state of mind, they often see those around them through the same critical filter we see ourselves through.

This "critical inner voice" is often directed at us, telling children that they are not good enough or will not fit in. Yet this inner critic's harsh judgement can be quickly reflected outwards on the people around a cynic child. They may tend to see someone from our closest friend to a distant relative solely because of their failures and fail to have compassion for their own problems and distractions. Since pessimistic and skeptical attitudes build a negative lens through which child view his environment, he tend to miss out on the joys in life when he is in this state.

They engage in a mentality of "us versus them" which pins us against some person or group. Distorting people is simple, and making a caricature of their faults. When we do this, it's worth asking ourselves, "Whose perspective is coming through? Is that how I really feel, or am I overreacting based on old feelings from my past?

" Such comparisons aren't always easy to make, but very often, our negative views mirror those of influential figures from our history. Such negativity can be infectious and can drag those around us down. It will cause us to alienate others, behave in a hostile way or become self-protective and alienated. In the end, being straightforward, unprotected and helpless is always in our own self-interest, rather than being mean or writing off men. The only person we are allowed to control is ourselves. When we become cynical we are the ones that are suffering.

8.3 Importance of Nurturing Child's Mind at Early Stage

They're developing brains. Experiences face by people in their early childhood have a profound effect on brain development— influencing learning, well-being, behavior, and, eventually, adult social relationships and earnings. Yet in the way we are trying to care for their bodies, we could do more to care for the young children's brains. Early years investment is one of the most effective and efficient investments a country can make to eradicate extreme poverty, improve shared prosperity, and build the human capital required to diversify and develop economies. The increasingly global digital world places even higher premiums on the capacities that derive from early childhood, such as the ability to reason, constantly learn, communicate effectively, and cooperate with others. Any people who don't early learn these skills and don't develop them through childhood and adolescence are likely to be left behind more. They know millions of young children are not achieving their full potential because of insufficient nutrition, lack of early stimulation, restricted early learning opportunities, and stress exposure.

Scientific findings from a variety of disciplines have demonstrated over the last three decades that the most critical elements of infant, adolescent, and adult health, well-being, and productivity take shape during the early years and especially the first 1000 days.

By the time a baby is born, the brain has all the cells and neurons, and by the age of two, massive numbers of neuronal connections are created that are later cut based on which they are most widely used The ideal environment encourages brain development, whereas a harmful climate inhibits growth in the short term but also in the long run.

Throughout pregnancy, for example, undernutrition, leading to low birth weight, increases the risk of chronic adult illnesses. Extreme poverty-related deprivation may result in reduced treatment by overworked, overwhelmed, and demoralized caregivers. The psychological and neurological growth of young children is compromised by constant trauma, without prospects for rehabilitation or healing.

Children who do not receive the treatment needed to enable their ability to quadruple, are less healthy, develop poorly, learn less, and achieve fewer grades at school, are more likely to have problems related to others with trust, and earn less as adults. As adults, they are expected to draw nearly a third less than their peers' average annual income without interference. It makes betting on their futures more difficult for them and their families, leading to crippling cycles of poverty between generations. Those individual costs aggregate throughout society, restricting the creation of wealth and eroding national earnings. As an outcome of the high level of pressure of weak early childhood growth and development, it is projected that some countries spend less on health than they are predicted to lose in the future. Fundamental learning skills and personal-social skills are learned at a young age, and the following qualifications are built upon these foundations. In the early years, preventive and promotive strategies accomplish more and cost less than later-age therapeutic approaches. In countries across the socio-economic spectrum, on-going studies show that nutritional and psycho-social programs introduced in the initial years of life have important benefits for health and well-being, employment and earnings, personal relationships, and social life.

9: Conclusion

Nurturing care consists of five components: wellness, education, safety and security, early learning, and sensitive treatment. Children need all five areas of nursing care to understand their capacity for success. Many health and nutrition programs, as well as safety and security policies, are already in place in many countries, but there is a need to expand their scope and efficiency. Their importance from birth to encourage the development of human capital should be recognized. The emphasis on early learning, responsive care, and the mental health of careers in the current framework is new. As we grow older, the brain becomes increasingly complex, and while new connections continue to be made, the brain is only built once, and under exceptional conditions. Nurturing care is the set of circumstances that provide the best care for young children. This refers to a stable environment created by parents and cares with help from policies, programs, and communities that ensures good health and nutrition for children, protects them from risks, provides them with opportunities for early learning through emotionally supportive and sensitive interactions. Nursing is essential for child development and lays the foundation for life-long health and well-being and creates human capital in today's child, tomorrow's adolescent and adult, and in the future into the next generation. For successful implementation of early childhood development policies, programs, and services, evaluation and transparency are essential to track threats, engagement, resources, and effects. Sound monitoring systems need to cover inputs, outputs, and results comprehensively, and be the responsibility of stakeholders across all industries. Data collection, interpretation, and reporting metrics, resources, and processes need to be made available and streamlined.

A catalyst for continuous improvement will be the regular compilation of relevant data in health and other programs, complemented by frequent in-depth and valid assessments.

Danish Way of Parenting

Discover the Parenting Secrets of the Happiest People in the World

By Samuel Pattinson

The trademarks that are used are without any consent, and the publication of the trademark is without permission or backing by the trademark owner. All trademarks and brands within this book are for clarifying purposes only and are the owned by the owners themselves, not affiliated with this document.

Introduction

Denmark, a small country in northern Europe known for the fairy tale by Hans Christian Andersen, The Little Mermaid, has been selected by the OECD (Organization for Economic Cooperation and Development) nearly every year since 1973 as the happiest people in the world. It's has been more than forty years since the happiest people in the world are regularly chosen! When you stop thinking about it for a second, it's a tremendous achievement. Even the latest United Nations Global Happiness Survey found Denmark at the top of the list every year since its launch. What is the secret to their success?

Countless papers and experiments were devoted to the resolution of this puzzle. Denmark? Denmark? What Denmark? Why Denmark? The documentary on this was entitled "The Discovery for Happiness" for 60 minutes. Oprah said, "Why are the Danes so happy?" And the findings are always inconclusive. Is it the scale of your social system, your houses or your government? It can't be high taxes, or the long, cold winters, so what does that give?

The United States, on the other hand, is not even among the top ten in its "pursuit of happiness" statement. It's just in the top 20, close to 17 after Mexico. Although we have a whole psychological area dedicated to the happiness and an infinite sea of self-help books, which tell us how to reach this mysterious condition, we are not so happy. Why is it? So, in fact, why are the Danes so happy?

I eventually discovered the secret of the Danes people. And the reason is in their upbringing, very obviously.

The Danish philosophy behind parenthood and their way of bringing up children produce some powerful results: resilient, emotionally safe, happy children who become resilient, emotionally secure and happy grown-ups who then reiterate this strong parenthood with their own children. The legacy is continued for over forty years.

Through exciting journey of discovery, I have decided to share with you this experience of the "Danish way." In this step-by-step guide, my goal is to help mothers and fathers who are about to start on or have started one of the most demanding and exceptional jobs in the world. It takes practice, persistence, determination and knowledge to implement this approach, but the results are worth the effort. Remember it's your legacy. Please read this book carefully if you want to create the happiest people in the world. The real secret to the prosperity of the Danes lies inside.

Chapter 1: Our Default Settings (P.A.R.E.N.T)

For time to time, we've all pondered what it takes to be a dad. Whether it's before your first child's birth, a kid's meltdown, or a fight over your kid's not eating his or her peas at the dinner table, and we've all once thought, "Do I do that right? "Many of us are pointing to books and the Internet, or we're looking about advice and support for friends and family. Most of us just want to be told we really do things the right way.

Yet hast thou ever considered what the right way is? Where do we get our ideas about parenting the right way? If you go to Italy at nine p.m., you'll see kids eating dinner. Running playing around in restaurants until nearly midnight; kids in Norway are routinely left outside in less than twenty degrees to sleep; running children in Belgium are allowed to drink beer. Some of these actions sound strange to us, but it's the "right" path for these people.

Such tacit agreed assumptions we have about how to raise our children are what Sara Harkness, a professor of human development at Connecticut University, calls "parental ethno-theories." She's been researching this phenomenon across societies for decades, and what she's discovered is that these fundamental views about the right way to parent are so rooted in our environment. It just seems to us like things are the way they are.

And so, most of us have been thinking about what being a parent means, but have you ever thought about what it means to be an American parent? About how we wear colorful American glasses and desire to see what is "the right way"?

What if we take off those glasses for a moment and would we see? If we stared back and looked away at the U.S., what would be our impression?

1.1 An Epidemic of Stress

I have seen a growing problem with the happiness level of people across the board. According to the National Center for Health Statistics, antidepressant have been used by 40% of American between 2005 and 2008. Kids are being treated with medicine and recommended for a growing number of psychological disorders, some with no specific diagnosis process. For 2010 alone, there were at least 5.2 million children taking Ritalin for attention deficit disorder between the ages of three and seventeen.

They are battling obesity and early puberty initiation, or "precocious adolescence," as it is now called. Girls and boys as young as seven and eight have testosterone injections pumped to delay the puberty. Most of us don't really doubt this as odd; rather, it's just the way things are. "My daughter gets the kill," one mother stressed around her eight-year-old, who she felt hit puberty too fast, nonchalantly.

Most adults, without even knowing it, are overly aggressive with themselves, their children and other people. Not all people are like that, of course, nor do they want to be, but they can also feel pressured to live in this aggressive society. The vocabulary around them can be loud and intimidating, putting people on the defensive:

"At soccer, Kim is just amazing. The coach says she is among the teams brightest. Yet despite basketball, karate and diving she still gets straight A's. How she does it, I don't care! What's Olivia up to? How do they do? "We feel pressure to perform to deliver with our children, to do well in school, and to satisfy our perception of what a good child should be, what a successful parent should be. The degree of uncertainty is often high, and we feel judged by others and by ourselves.

This is part of human nature, and part of that is what it is to be American. What pushes us as a society to perform and compete, and be successful to a standard that does not ultimately seem to make us as adults very happy? What if some of the "answers" that we have are faulty to raise our children our parenting norms?

What if we discovered the glasses we wore had the wrong prescription, and we couldn't see things as clearly as we thought? We'd remove the glasses, fix our view and look at our planet again. We'd come across things looking different! The question arises simply when attempting to see life from a new perspective, through new lenses: Is there a better way?

Maria's and Joseph Story

I discovered from my friend Maria and from her Danish husband Joseph a philosophy of raising children which opened my eyes and completely changed my life. Happy children grow up into happy adults raising happy children, and so on. My good friend Joseph and I have been discussing the proposal. Joseph is a Danish psychotherapist with many years of experience working with families and children and we asked the question together: "Is there a Danish way of parenting?" To her knowledge, that was not the case. For some literature on the subject we looked high and low but there was nothing. She had never heard of a "Danish Way" during all her years of working in the Danish school system and being a family psychotherapist. She knew all the academic theories and research into parenting practices, many of which she used on a daily basis in her family life, but could there be a distinctive parenting style embedded in her very own culture that she had not seen?

1.2 Examining Our "Default Settings"

The other day Maria and her almost-three-year-old son were in the area. He was on a push-bike with no brakes, so he began pushing himself out into the street amid her several crying to him to stop. She ran frenzied after him, grabbing him by the neck and shaking him. She has been we sometimes forget that parenting is a verb, like love.

Furious and afraid, and he was about to scream, "If I tell you to stop, you'd better stop!" Maria could see that she was going to cry out of panic, and at that time, it took all her courage to collect the energy to go out and see what she was doing. She did not want to react like that. She scanned her mind for a different way, and there was an answer, miraculously. She paused, took a breath, and lowered to his floor. She held his arms and imploringly stared into his eyes. She said in a calm but concerned voice, "Want to go ow-ow? Mum doesn't want to go ow-ow! Look at those cars? "She was looking at the vehicles and smiling." Ow-ow cars go to Sebastian! "He smiled, then waited. "Motorcars. Ow-ow,' he repeated.

"That's how you stop when Mommy says to stop, Ok? So that you don't leave the cars ow-ow. "He nodded. In the end, he did not cry. They kissed, and Maria could sense on her shoulder, smiling at him. "Motorcars. Ow-ow. "They'd been at another crosswalk five minutes later. Maria kept telling him to stop, and he did. He pointed to the lane, shaking his head. "Cars ow-ow." She told him how pleased she was when she stood and knocked.

Not only was she pleased with him for leaving, you see. She was also happy with herself for stopping for stopping herself in a difficult moment and changing her natural behavior, her default settings. It wasn't easy, but doing so turned a tense and potentially explosive situation into a happy and secure one, and the outcome made both of them happier.

They occasionally forget that parenting is a verb, like marriage. To yield positive returns, it requires effort and work. Being a good parent requires an incredible amount of self-awareness. This demands that we look at what we are doing when we are tired and stressed and strained to our limits. Such behaviors are considered our "normal settings." The actions and reactions we have are our default settings when we are too lazy to choose a better way.

Our parents inherit most of our default settings. They're drilled into us and programmed like a machine motherboard. These are the industrial environments that we resort to when we are at the edge of our wit and not thinking; our culture has built them within us. It is when we hear ourselves saying things that we really don't want to be doing. It is when we behave and respond in situations that we aren't aware that we want to act and react. It's when we feel bad, and we know deep down that there's an easier way to get results from our babies, but we're not sure what it is. Anyone who has children understands the feeling.

That's why looking at the default settings, learning them and knowing them, is so critical. What do you like about how you interact with your children and how you react? What is it you don't like? What do you do is just a continuation of your own upbringing? What is it you want to change? And when you see what your parent's natural inclinations are your favorite settings can you determine how you want them to change for the better.

We'll allow you to see what some of those positive changes can be in the chapters that follow. Using the easy-to-remember acronym PARENT play, authenticity, reframing, empathy, no ultimatums, and juxtaposition we'll examine some of the tried-and-true methods that have been working for parents in Denmark for over 40 years.

Increasing our awareness of ourselves and taking conscious decisions about our actions and reactions are the first steps towards a powerful change in life. So we're better parents and better people. And this is how we build a well-being culture that can be carried on to the next generations. Is there a bigger gift you can bestow on your children than helping them grow up healthier? Healthy and more resilient adults? We don't believe that. So we believe that you will agree.

Chapter 2: Play

2.1 P Is for Play

Have you found that the urge to coordinate events for your children is unspoken, or even spoken? Whether it's the pool, dance, T-ball, or soccer, if you don't have your kids sign up for at least three to four events a week, you just don't feel like you're doing your job. However, many times do you hear parents say they take up their Saturday by taking their children to various sports, lessons, or activities?

In comparison, when was the last time you heard anyone say, "My daughter will be playing on Saturday"?

And by "play," we don't mean playing the violin or playing a sport, or even going to a playdate where adults arrange events. We say "play" in which they are left to their own devices, with a partner or alone, to play for as long as they want, just as they see fit. And even though parents allow this free play to take place, there is often a nagging sense of guilt to accept it. Because in the end, we feel we're better parents by teaching them something, involving them in a sport, or giving some input to their little brains. Gaming often seems like a waste of worthwhile learning time. But are they?

The number of hours children are allowed to play in the United States in the past fifty years has dramatically decreased. Aside from TV and electronics, there is also the concern of parents that children will get injured combined with a need to "create" them all these considerations take much of the opportunity they once had to play.

As parents, when our children show visible signs of progress, we feel comforted. Parents like to watch them play soccer while others egg them on, or go to their piano or dance recitals. We're proud to say Billy won a medal or prize, or learned a new tune, or can read the Spanish alphabet. It makes us feel good parents. They do it with the best intentions, as they give them more guidance and organized opportunities and teach them to become more positive, productive people. Or do we?

The prevalence of anxiety disorders, insomnia, and concentration issues has skyrocketed in the U.S. is no wonder. Is it true that we leave our kids nervous by not encouraging them to play more without knowing it?

Are we over Programming Our Kids' Lives?

Most parents aim to get their kids started early at school or skip a grade. Children learn to read and do math's earlier and earlier, and we are proud that they are "smart" and that being smart or athletic is highly valued in American culture. Through tutors and fun equipment and programmers, we can go to great lengths to try to get them there. Progress is progress, and these signs are real, noticeable and observable. Free play sounds enjoyable for all intents and purposes but what does it actually tell them?

What if we told you free play gave kids less anxiety? It imparts endurance to them. Yet endurance has proved to be one of the key factors in forecasting success as an adult. In a healthy, functioning adult, the ability to "bounce back," regulate emotions and cope with stress is a key trait. They now know that resilience is important to avoid anxiety and depression, and for years, the Danes have been instilling it in their children. And one way they've done, that is by putting a lot of focus on the story.

In Denmark, which dates back to 1871, husband and wife Niels and Erna Juel-Hansen came up with the first developmental theory-based pedagogy that integrated play. We found that free play is important to the development of a child. In reality, Danish kids were not even allowed to begin school for many years before they were seven. Instructors and people who set the agenda for children's schools didn't want them to get involved in education because they felt kids should be kids, and play first and foremost.

Even now, at two p.m., children are ten years old, and regular school is under completion. And then have the option of going to what is known as "free-time school" (skolefritidsordning) for the rest of the day, where they are often encouraged to play. Splendid but real!

Throughout Denmark, the focus is not exclusively on schooling or sports but on the whole child. Parents and teachers concentrate on things such as socialization, individuality, unity, equality and self-esteem. We want their kids to learn endurance and to grow a strong inner compass to lead them through life. We know that their children will be well educated and that they will learn other skills. Yet true happiness doesn't only come from a good education. A kid who learns to cope with stress makes friends, and yet is pragmatic about the future, for instance, has a set of life skills which are very different from being a math genius. And the Danes speak about all aspects of life through life skills, not just work-life. For what is a master in mathematics without being able to cope with the ups and downs of life? All the Danish parents we talked to have said they find it very odd to rely constantly on bullying young children.

As they see it, if children are always performing to get something good grades, awards, or praise from teachers or parents then they're not getting their inner drive developed.

We believe that children fundamentally need room and confidence to allow them to learn issues on their own, to build and solve their own problems. It promotes genuine self-esteem and self-reliance because it comes from someone else's own internal cheerleader of the kid.

2.2 Internal vs. External Locus of Control

In psychology, this internal cheerleader or drive is called the control locus. In Latin, the word locus means "place" or "location," and thus the locus of control simply refers to the degree to which a person feels he has a sense of control over his own life and the events that affect him. Thus, persons with an internal control locus believe they have the power to control their lives and the things that happen to them. Their drive is internal, or personal; from within comes their place of control. Those with an external locus of control assume that external factors such as the world or destiny control their lives, which they have no power over, regulate. That makes them arrives from without, so they can't change it. We are all influenced by our environment, history, and social status, but the distinction between internal and external locus of control is how much we believe we can control our lives given those influences.

Research has shown consistently that infants, teenagers, and adults with a high external control locus are predisposed to anxiety and depression they become nervous when they feel they have little or no control over their life, and they become distressed when that sense of helplessness becomes too intense.

Research also shows that in the last fifty years, there has been a dramatic shift toward a more centralized influence locus for young people.

Psychologist Jean M. Twenge and colleagues looked over a fifty-year period for results from a test called the Children's Nowicki-Strickland Internal-External Control Scale. This test measures whether an individual has an inside or an outside control locus. The researchers found that in children of all ages, from primary school to college, there was a dramatic shift from an internal to an external locus of control. To give you an idea of how great a shift it was, in 1960, youth were 80 per cent more likely to claim that parents in Denmark would not try to intervene unless it was absolutely necessary.

They had control over their lives in 2002 compared with children who were more likely to say they lacked such personal control.

And what was even more striking being that the trend for elementary school kids was more pronounced than for middle and college kids. So there is a loss of control over their lives with younger and younger girls. Earlier and earlier, they experience a sense of helplessness. Over the years, this rise in external control locus has a linear correlation with the rise of depression and anxiety in our society. What could this change cause?

Giving Kids the Space to Learn and Grow

A concept called "proximal growth" is fundamental to the Danish parenting philosophy, first proposed by the Russian developmental psychologist Lev Vygotsky. It basically states that, with the right amount of help, a child needs the right amount of space to learn and grow in the ways that suit him or her.

Consider helping a child climb a fallen log in the forests. If he needs a hand at first, you give a hand, but then maybe just a finger to help him over, and when the time is right, you let him go. You don't move him or pull him over.

Parents in Denmark seek not to interfere unless it is absolutely necessary. Parents trust their kids to be able to do and try new things and give them room to develop their own self-confidence. In their growth, parents provide them with scaffolding to help them build their self-esteem, which is very necessary for the "whole person." When children feel so stressed, they will lose the excitement in what they do, and this can lead to fear and anxiety. Instead, Danish parents try to meet kids where they feel safe trying a new talent, then encourage them and invite them to go further or try something new while it still feels fun and strange.

Having this room and maintaining the proximal growth zone helps children to develop both maturity and confidence in their internal control locus as they know that they are in charge of their own problems and progress. Kids who are forced or pulled too much fear having an unconscious feedback locus because they do not control their development; then, there are external factors, and the foundation for their self-esteem is weak.

They often believe they help kids by forcing them to succeed or learn faster, but leading them in the right moment in their growth will produce even better results not only because of the learning itself, which will certainly be more pleasurable but because the kids will be more confident of the mastering of their talents because they are more in control of gaining them.

British researcher David Elkind agrees. For example, children who are forced to read earlier can read better than their peers at first, but those rates even out in a couple of years ' time and at what cost? In the long run, forced kids show higher levels of anxiety and lower self-esteem.

In the U.S., we find endless books on how fear and depression can be raising or diminished.

They want to reduce tension at all costs for our children in particular. Most parents helicopter over their kids and interfere with securing them at the time of the moment. Most of us are barricading staircases and securing and locking up anything we might find remotely dangerous. If we don't, we sound like we're bad parents and we're actually judging and being criticized by others for not doing enough to defend them. Many days need so many gizmos and inventions to be covered that one wonders how twenty years ago, children survived.

Not only do we want to protect our kids from tension, but we also want to develop their self-confidence and make them feel special too. The standard method of doing so is to congratulate them for trivial accomplishments, even unnecessarily. But in our attempt to increase confidence and reduce stress, in the long term, we could simply set them up for more stress. Creating self-esteem rather than trust is like making a nice house with little base. We both know what happens when the wolf arrives big bad.

But How Can Play Help?

For years, scientists have studied playing in animals, trying to understand its evolutionary purpose. So one thing they find is that gaming is key to understanding how to cope with stress. In studies done on domestic rats and rhesus monkeys, scientists found that these animals were stressed out as adults when they were deprived of playmates during a critical stage in their development. We would overreact to challenging situations and couldn't manage social settings well. They would either respond with extreme terror, fleeing often trembling into a corner or with intense anger, lashing out in frustration. The lack of play was probably the culprit, as they behaved more naturally and coped better as adults when the animals were allowed a playmate for even an hour a day.

Fight-or-flight behaviors that are normally experienced in play activate the same neurochemical brain pathways as stress. When you see dogs running around chasing each other for fun, think about it. Most animals participate in this kind of play, taking the position of subordinate or antagonist in a play fight, causing some form of tension. We know that introducing baby animals ' brains to stress affects them in a way that makes them less susceptible to stress over time, making their brains better at controlling stress as they mature. Their ability to cope is constantly improving by play, and they are able to deal with increasingly difficult circumstances. You see, endurance isn't developed by escaping pain, but by learning how to master and control it.

Should we strip away the ability of our children to control the tension by not permitting them to play enough? Looking at the number of anxiety disorders in our culture and diagnosis of depression, one asks if something is wrong. As one of someone with an anxiety disorder's biggest reported fears is losing control over one's emotions, we can't help but ask: if we stand back and let our kids play more, will they be more resilient and happier adults? We believe that the answer is yes.

2.3 Play and Coping Skills

In a pilot study carried out at a child development center in Massachusetts on preschool children, researchers wanted to measure whether there was a positive correlation between the level of playfulness in preschoolers and their coping skills. Using a playfulness test and a coping inventory,

the investigators cross-checked the playfulness of the children and the quality of their coping skills.

What they observed was a direct positive link between the level of playfulness in children and their ability to cope. The more they played the more they got to learn social skills and engage in social / play contexts the more they coped. This prompted the researchers to conclude that playing had a direct impact on all their ability to adapt to life.

Another research, conducted by Professor Louise Hess of occupational therapy and colleagues at a health center in Palo Alto, California, sought to explore the association between playfulness and coping skills in adolescent boys. We also researched young boys naturally and those with emotional issues. As in the analysis of childhood, there was a strong and important link between the degree of playfulness and their ability to cope for both classes of students. The researchers concluded that play could be used to enhance coping skills, especially the ability to adapt and more flexibly approach issues and goals.

That does make sense. Look outside just to see kids swinging from the bars or climbing trees or jumping from the top. We are monitoring dangerous situations, and nobody knows the right dosage or how to treat it but the kid himself. But it's important that they feel the dose of stress they can handle is in control. That in itself makes them feel better at managing their lives. The same is true of young animals and primates. We deliberately put themselves in dangerous situations, diving and hanging from trees as we twist and turn to make it difficult to land. We hear about anxiety and how to cope with it. As mentioned earlier, it is the same as the battle for games. To understand the emotional complexities of both, the animals put themselves in both the subordinate and the intruder roles.

Socio-situations are also overwhelming for youngsters. Social play will offer rivalry as well as teamwork. Fear and anger are just a few of the feelings a kid has to learn to cope with in order to continue playing.

There is no such thing in play as receiving undue acclaim. Regulations need to be discussed and renegotiated, and players need to be mindful of the other players ' mental state to avoid someone getting upset and leaving, and if too many players leave, the game is over. Since children simply want to play with each other, these situations require them to practice getting along with others as equals a critical later life ability for satisfaction.

Play is so important to the Danish concept of youth that many Danish schools have programs in place to allow all students to learn by activities, play, and exercise. For starters, Play Patrol focuses on the younger elementary school students and is encouraged by the older ones. These student-led programs encourage young and older students to play various activities such as hide-and-seek, firefighter, or pet family and encourage shy, lonely children to join the game as well. For different age groups, this form of enjoyable and imaginative play allows children to test themselves in a way they don't want with their parents or teachers. This significantly reduces bullying and fosters social skills and self-control.

The Truth behind Lego and Playgrounds

Almost everyone has heard of Lego and has played at least once in their lives with the iconic colorful building blocks. At the turn of the millennium, Lego, apparently one of the most famous toys in existence, was dubbed "the invention of the century" by Fortune magazine. Initially made of wood, Lego has never forgotten its simple understanding of building blocks. Like the proximal construction region, Lego will work for all ages. When the kid is willing to take the next step towards a more difficult building, Legos are designed for that. It's a perfect way to play with your child and help her slowly learn a new level. She will play on her own or with friends; she has spent countless hours playing with Lego around the globe.

Many people don't know about Lego the interesting fact is that it's from Denmark. Built-in 1932 by a Danish carpenter in his studio, it was dubbed Lego as a contraction of the words leg godt, meaning "play well." Even then, the notion of openly using creativity was in full bloom.

Another of the largest play facilitator providers in the world is another Danish company named Kompan. This produces natural playgrounds that have received multiple architecture awards in favor of children's play for their usability, consistency and functionality. The organization's mission has been to promote healthy play as important to children's learning. His first park was unintentionally built more than forty years ago when a young Danish artist found that his colorful art installation, which was designed to brighten up a drab housing complex, was used more by children to play on than by adults.

Kompan is now the world's number one manufacturer to the playground. It's interesting and quite revealing that the world leader in both indoor and outdoor play equipment is a nation of just five million people.

And note that this is their way of learning how much tension they will handle the next time you see your kids swing from the trees, leap off some rocks or play fighting with their mates and you want to try to save them. If they play in a group with some tough kids and you want to defend them, note that they are developing self-control and negotiating skills to keep the game alive with all sorts of different personalities. That is their way to test their own abilities and improve process adaptability skills. The more they play, the more resilient they become and become socially adept. It is an incredibly natural process. The building block for the construction of an empire of future happiness is able to leg godt or "play well."

2.4 Tips for Play

- Turn the TV and the electronics off! Imagination is an essential ingredient for the positive effects of play.

- Creating an enriching environment Studies show that a sensory-rich environment combined with play allows the brain to expand cortically. Using a variety of materials in which all the senses can be stimulated visual, auditory, tactile, etc. improves brain development through practice.

- Using creativity to expand the minds of children when they do make art. So don't teach them how to do it just set out the art supplies and let them spontaneously make them.

- Let them explore outdoors. Get them out to play in nature as much as possible the forests, the forest, the beach, wherever they may be. Try to find safe areas where you have no doubt of letting them be open and explore the world. These are ways they can use their imaginations and really have fun.

- Mix children of different ages try matching your kids with kids of different ages. This strengthens the proximal growth region, allowing one to promote learning for the other, ultimately encouraging each to reach a new level. Children learn to both lead in the game as well as work with older ones in this way. We learn to take part and contest the game as well. It teaches the necessary skills of self-control and persuasion in life.

- Let them be safe to forget the shame that they don't need any experience or unique toys guided by adults. The more you can let them have power over their own games, use their creativity, and do it on their own, the better they will get at it. The skills which they learn are invaluable. We are so caught up in thinking about how many organized activities our kids are involved in, or what they are talking about, that we forget the importance of encouraging them to play safe. Stop feeling guilty about letting them play does not mean you're a dad. All they miss is free play!

- Be true. If you want to play with your baby, in what you do, you have to be 100 per cent honest. Don't worry about looking foolish. Let them guide. Don't care what people think of you, or what you think of yourself. Sit down to their level and try letting go for just twenty minutes a day if that's hard for you. Even at their stage, a little playtime is worth more than any gift you might purchase.

- Let them play on their own to Playing alone is extremely important to children. It's often a way of processing new experiences, disagreements and daily things of their life as they play with their toys. We will re-enact what is happening in their imagination, which is incredibly relaxing, by engaging in fantasy play and using different voices. It's perfect for building their creativity and fantasy too.
- Build an obstacle course. Try to build obstacle courses using tiny stools and mattresses, or create space in the house by any other way so that children can run about and use their creativity. Let them play and climb and experiment and build freely and don't sweat it over.

- Get other parents involved in the movement for safe play. The more parents who do it, the freer the children can engage in non-adult-led games together. In the United States, podiatrists have established recommendations to reassure parents that playing is safe. It is fun for youth and should be promoted and shared with others.

- Do not intervene too fast. Try not to judge the other children too harshly and intervene too quickly because you want to protect your children from others. Sometimes it's learning how to deal with the tougher kids that provide them with the biggest lessons on self-control and endurance.

- Let your kids do things themselves. Just step back and take a breath when you feel the need to "save" them. Know they master some of the essential talents to help them through life.

Chapter 3: Authenticity

3.1 A Is for Authenticity

Have you ever watched a happy ending movie that didn't really make you feel good? One in which you found, despite the great resolution, that you had the feeling somewhere deep inside yourself that your life wasn't so perfect? Wasn't your job terrific? Your friendship, home, car or clothes just weren't as good as the ones in the movie? Hadn't the whole thing really felt that realistic? Yet you set it aside because it was, after all, a feel-good movie, so there's no need to talk about it too much. Many Hollywood movies are supposed to get you feeling good. But when art imitates life, you wonder how realistic these syrupy-sweet endings are in fact.

In comparison, very often, Danish films have dreary, grim, or dramatic ends. Much rarer is one left with the happy endings we're used to. Maria has watched Danish films countless times and waited to hear the calming background music that would signal that her misery was about to stop and that after all, everything would work out well. The kid would get the girl, the hero would save the day, and the world would all be perfect. She almost felt like an American it was her right to have a happy ending. But the Danish films would focus upon delicate, actual, and painful topics time and time again that didn't tie it up with a nice bow. On the opposite, with their raw emotions triggered and unfinished, they left Maria and its fellow audience members behind. How could Danes be so happy watching films like this?

Communications professor Silvia Knobloch-Westerwick and colleagues at Ohio State

University have done research that has shown that, contrary to popular belief, seeing dramatic or sad movies often makes people happier by drawing attention to some of the more positive aspects of their own lives. This tends to make people think with appreciation and empathy on their own relationships, making them happier and more in harmony with our own humanity.

Fairy-tale Endings

Hans Christian Andersen is perhaps one of the best known Danish writers in history. He is the author and forefather of many fairy tales like "The Little Mermaid," "The Ugly Duckling," and "The Emperor's New Clothes," to name but a few. These are tales which were told throughout the world. But what most people don't realize is that there are many original fairy tales by Andersen that don't have our idea of a fairy-tale ending at all. They are dramas. As an example, the Little Mermaid does not get the prince but instead, due to sadness, transforms into sea foam. Many of the fairy tales by Andersen were merely tailored to fit our cultural ideal of how things should be.

In the English translations of Andersen's fairy tales, parents paid close attention to what they felt children should be spared from reading. For Denmark and the older versions, it is more up to the authors to come up with their own assumptions and decisions. Danes think that tragedies and upsetting events are also things we should be talking about. From our sufferings, we learn more about character than from our successes; therefore, it is important to look into all parts of life. This is more authentic, creating empathy and more profound respect for humanity. It also makes us feel gratitude for the ordinary things in our lives that we sometimes take for granted when relying too much on fairy-tale life.

Authenticity for the Danes starts with an awareness of our own emotions. When we teach our children to recognize and accept their real emotions, good or bad, and act in a way that's consistent with their beliefs, the struggles and rough patches of life won't undermine them. We should know that they have acted in accordance with what feels right. We should learn how to understand their own boundaries and value them. This internal compass, authentic value-based self-esteem, becomes the leading force in one's life, essentially immune to external pressures.

3.2 Parenting with Authenticity

Parenting with honesty is the first step to leading children to be courageously true to themselves and others. Being a model of emotional health is effective parenting. Emotional honesty, not perfection, is what children really need from their parents. Kids are always watching how you feel anger, happiness, disappointment, contentment, and accomplishment and how you express it in the world. We have to model authenticity for our children and let them know that it is OK to express all of their emotions. Most parents find it easier to handle their children's happy feelings, but when it comes to the more challenging ones, such as frustration, hostility, and fear, it becomes more difficult. As a result, children learn less about these feelings, which may affect their ability to control them in the future. Acknowledging and embracing all feelings, including hard ones, makes it easier to navigate in the world at an early stage.

When you go through a difficult time, for example, laughing and pretending that everything is OK is not always the best course of action. Self-deception is the worst kind of deceit and is a risky transmitting message to our children. They'll have to do likewise. Self-deception is misleading because it allows us to disregard our real feelings and may allow us to make

choices based on external factors rather than our own honest wishes. It takes us down roads to points in life that we don't really want to be. And that is how sad we end up.

It's that time when many people are looking at their life and thinking, "Hold tight, is this really what I wanted? Or was that what I felt I would ask for? "Authenticity, on the other hand, checks your heart and intestines for what is best for you and your children and is not afraid to follow it through. This helps you to be in contact with your own feelings, and move on them instead of suppressing them or numbing them. These things take courage and strength, but there's a huge payoff. Trying to focus on intrinsic desires, such as strengthening relationships or investing in activities that you enjoy, rather than on extrinsic goals, such as buying a new car, is what helps to create true well-being.

So it can be a self-deceptive pitfall to have a bigger house or more things or to engage the children in all the right sports. Instead of listening carefully to their wishes and respecting their unique pace of growth and development, pushing your own or other dreams onto your children is another pitfall. Children may learn to do things for outward attention rather than for inner gratification, which becomes a default setting for life because they are too stressed or rewarded. It encourages extrinsic goals: To make them happy, they need something outside of themselves. This can bring success by the standards of some people, but it will not necessarily bring them that deep sense of inner happiness and well-being that we are all striving for. It can potentially cause anxiety and depression, as we have seen earlier.

3.3 The Danish Way of Authentic Praise

In Denmark, humbleness is a very important value. This dates back long into history and is part of the cultural heritage of the Danes. This value of humility is about knowing who you are so well that to make you feel important. You don't need others. So they're trying not to flood their kids with compliments.

Joseph often tells her daughters that with hard work they can do whatever. They know they need to develop and grow, and she supports that.

Yet she attempts not to overpraise them, realizing that too many compliments can't make sense for kids because they can sound empty and hollow.

For e.g., if a Danish boy scribes a drawing really quickly and sends it to her father, the parent will probably not say, "Wow! Good job! You are such a good performer! "She has a greater chance of thinking about the drawing itself. "What are they? "When you wrote this, what were you talking about? "Why did you use colors like that? "Or maybe she'd just say thank you if it were a gift.

Focusing on the task is a much more Danish approach, rather than complimenting the child too much. It tends you focus on the work done, which encourages modesty as well. Helping children build on the feeling that they are capable of mastering a skill rather than being a master provides a more solid foundation from which to stand and grow. That encourages endurance and inner strength.

And, in reality, this concept is backed by new and fascinating work. The way we treat our children has a profound effect on resilience!

Fixed Mind-set vs. a Growth Mind-set

In the U.S., many parents believe that rewarding children for their intellect build their trust and learning motivation. American parents tend to complement their children and others openly and feel it increases their faith and growth. Yet three decades of Stanford psychologist Carol S. Deck's work has proven otherwise.

Praise is intimately related to how children perceive their intellect. Children acquire what is considered a "locked" mind-set (their intellect is predetermined, and they have it) if they are continually rewarded for being inherently clever, creative, or gifted (sound familiar?).

In comparison, children who are advised they should improve their knowledge through work and education develop a mentality of development (they can develop their talents because they are working very hard).

Dweck's findings show that children with a fixed mindset, who have been constantly told they're clever, seem to be obsessed first and foremost with how they're going to be judged: smart or not. We are scared of having to expend too much effort because we feel stupid with effort. They think you shouldn't have to put effort into this if you have the potential. So since they have always been assured that they have the skill, they are scared that they will lose their status as "smart" by having to really try hard to do something. Kids with that mindset tend to care about studying, instead. Those inspired to rely on their efforts rather than their intellect see the initiative as a positive thing. This stimulates and encourages their intellect to rise. Such students are growing their attempts in the face of disappointment and looking for new ways in learning, rather than giving up. This is the durability epitome.

3.4 The Key to Lifelong Learning and Success

Growing research in psychology and neuroscience also supports the notion that growth mentality is the real catalyst for exceptional achievement. Brain studies indicate that over time, our consciousness has far more plasticity than we ever dreamed of. Through learning even into old age, the fundamental facets of our intellect can be increased. When faced with challenges, it's patience and determination that are the key ingredients of overall success in many fields.

That really is an eye-opener. How many smart and talented people do you know who never lived up to their potential because they had a predetermined mindset of being inherently clever so they stopped trying when success didn't come easily?

Several fascinating research by Dweck and collaborators on fifth-graders tried to see how the recognition influences the success of the pupils. Student groups were given specific assignments to work on, and then received various kinds of praise for their efforts. Several students heard things like "You must be clever to solve these problems" (encouraging a fixed mindset) and others heard "You must have worked hard to solve these problems" (encouraging the mindset). Afterwards, the students were asked to agree or disagree with some comments, such as "The intellect is something fundamental about you that you can't really alter." Students who were rewarded for being clever agreed with these statements much more than those who were congratulated for their initiative.

The students have been asked to give their definition of intelligence in a follow-up report. Those praised for intellect said they thought it was a set innate trait, whereas those praised for the initiative said it was something you could improve with training.

Afterwards, students were given the option to work on a simple or complicated problem. The students who have been lauded for intellect have preferred to do the easier question rather than the challenging one, possibly in order to ensure a perfect result. The ones lauded for the initiative have selected the difficult one with the chance to learn.

All the students were eventually given a complicated task to focus on. The children with fixed mind-set lost their confidence and happiness the minute they had difficulty solving the problem. The promotion meant being innately clever for them, and fighting meant that they did not.

On the other hand, the children with that mindsets did not lose their faith and were eager to try to solve the problem.

When the challenge was made easier again, the students appreciated the fact that their intellect had already lost their confidence and motivation in the hardest question and had gone badly overall. As a group, they fared worse on the same sort of mission they had been assigned at the outset, while the community appreciated their continued improvement in their performance and did an excellent job overall.

Perhaps the most interesting thing, however, was that when asked anonymously to submit their ratings, set minds over reported their results more than 40% of the time. Their self-image was so tied up with their ratings that they were reluctant to admit defeat, while the development mind-sets changed their scores upward by 10% of the time. Research on bullying in schools suggests that now, pupils are much more likely to cheat in order to get high grades than in previous generations, a result of intensified pressure to achieve combined, in many situations, with a fixed mindset.

They think telling kids how brilliant they are improving their morale, but it actually makes them lose confidence in the face of difficulties! Praising students for their intellect doesn't give them the critical incentive or stamina to be successful, but can give them a fixed, fragile mindset instead. Conversely, appreciation for commitment or "process" praise for dedication, perseverance, tactics, progress, etc. fosters inspiration and resilience. It highlights what they have done to be successful for children and what they need to do to be successful in the future.

Ironically, a recent article in the New York Times notes that even companies today look for people with a mentality of development rather than a fixed attitude.

Since individuals with an increasing mentality are better at promoting collaboration and overcoming problems without getting stressed out, they are much more appealing to most organizations. The innately creative, or predetermined mindsets, are more egocentric and concerned about being the organization's biggest star. It's the people who can handle a challenge with perseverance and persistence, attracting thankful friends, who will finally get the coveted position and even making it into CEO level.

Some examples of process praise:

"I like the way you tried to put together the pieces of the puzzle over and over again. You have not given up and have found a way to pull it together! "You have performed this dance so many times and today's dedication has really been seen! You danced so right! "How you shared your snack with your dad, I am so proud of you. It makes me so happy to see you sharing." "It's been a long, challenging task, but you stayed at it and got it done.

3.5 Tips for Authenticity

- Weed out self-deception in the first place be frank with yourself. Know how to look authentically at your own personality. It is a huge milestone to be able to detect and define your own emotions and how you feel really. It is a great gift to teach your children emotional honesty and to prevent them from becoming self-deceptive. Hearing one's own true thoughts and feelings and expressing them is what keeps us on the right path to follow what makes us happy in life. It's how we calibrate our inner compasses, to be frank with ourselves and place ourselves in the right direction.
- Respond frankly if your children ask a question, then give them an honest answer. Your responses will, of course, be age-appropriate and proportionate to their level of understanding. In all aspects of life, it is important, to be honest in your answers, even the tough ones. You are weakening the child's ability to know what is true and false by not being truthful.

- Using stories from your own life, whether it's a doctor's office or a difficult situation or just a fun time, kids like to hear about your experiences and how you feel when you were little, particularly when it's genuine and heartfelt. It gives them a better sense of who you are, which helps them to realize that even if they are afraid, happy or sad, their condition is normal.

- Teach integrity Talk to your kids about the value of honesty within your family. Render an interest to it. Let them know why you value integrity more than punishment for bad behavior. When you threaten your children with indignation or accusations accusingly and are harsh when they misbehave, they may be scared, to tell the truth. They'll be honest if you make it safe for them. Remember, it takes a lot for anyone at any age to confess or tell the truth. Apparently, it isn't always coming. It is up to us to encourage them to be bold enough to be truthful and insecure and to apologize if needed. Be non-committal. When fostered well, this kind of honest relationship will be of paramount importance during teenage years.

- Write stories expressing all emotions. Tell stories of all sorts to your kids. Don't worry if not all of them have happy endings. Actively select tales that also have difficult subjects, and stories that don't finish in a "storybook" way.

- Kids learn a lot from grief and loss (being of course age-appropriate), and they open up honest communication with you on different aspects of life that are just as important as the prince had the princess. Exposure to life's peaks and valleys fosters empathy, endurance and feelings of meaningfulness and appreciation for our own lives.

- Use process praise Keep in mind that the most meaningful and useful praise is based on quality, not quantity.

Hold your attention based on the method or initiative that children put in rather than on innate abilities: "You've studied hard for your exam, and your progress reflects that. Multiple times you walked over the material, made cue cards and questioned yourself. That did work! "Try to come up with some more Process Louise examples. Practice makes things perfect the more you try to use the praise of the process, the better you get it. See if you can avoid saying, "You're so smart." By focusing on the effort involved, you'll give your kids the tools to understand that what matters most is perseverance, not an innate ability. In the long run, because of it, they will have greater self-esteem.

- Do not use praise as a default response. Do not exaggerate appreciation for items that are too simple. This can teach your child that when he performs a mission quickly, easily, and beautifully, he's just praiseworthy and that doesn't inspire him to take on tasks. When, for instance, a child quickly gets an A without much effort, try saying, "Well that was too easy for you! Why don't we try to do something more demanding, from which you can learn? "The goal is not to make quickly completed things the basis for our admiration.

- Reflect on effort and hold it sincere be quick of credit for errors or shortcomings. Saying such things as "Well done! "You've done your best! "Next time, better luck! "Can be heard pitifully. Focus on what they did and how it can be accomplished "I know you missed the goal, but it was very close! Let's get out next week and practice so you'll get it next time! The practice is important, remember! "By concentrating on the learning effort, we build a mentality of development. This collection of minds is useful in all aspects of life, from work to interactions.

- Teach kids not to equate themselves with others. They need to know if they have done their best on a project or if they like they can do more. Not everyone can be the best at all, but for yourself, you can be the best. This emphasis fosters health as opposed to competition with others.

- Highlight your own and honest viewpoint, and that of your child, by saying "for me" Try to add "for me" after a statement to reinforce the awareness that your perception of a given situation is not exactly the same as that of your child. For example, if you have a disagreement with your child that food is too hot, consider that although it isn't too hot for you, it might be too hot for her. Saying, "I don't think the food is too spicy for me," let her know you appreciate this. Or instead of saying, "The weather isn't cool," you might say, "The weather isn't cold for me." This appreciation for the individual experience builds confidence and reverence which helps children understand and appreciate their own experience.

Chapter 4: Reframing

4.1 R Is for Reframing

AS an American marrying a Dane, Maria recalls the first time she learned that her husband was doing something for their children differently than what she was. She tended to respond a little too quickly whenever there was a negative situation of some sort. She'd throw her hands up with exasperation. "We are not going to do it! She would never listen! "Meanwhile, her husband always had more courage, more grace, and a magical expression on hand for every circumstance that even Maria could be astonished. It was like a window opening into a darkened room, throwing new light on a conversation in which she had not seen any potential before. He might place a more positive light on something negative. He might make a black-and-white situation appear a bit greyer. Pain became less intense and more balanced with rage. Maria thought his family and friends were doing the same for their families. Where was this magical book of phrases used by these Danes?

One moment, listening to her husband delicately change the vocabulary of their daughter around her fear of spiders, it struck Maria just how important that effect would have been for the life of her family. When she watched her daughter study the spider closely with him and marvel at it, rather than crying in terror and shouting, "Eew!" It struck her that it was extremely important to use the" Danish style "of expression. Because it wasn't just the language; it was about using the language to create a shift in perception.

Taking Off Your Old Glasses (again)

You know, the way we see life and process our daily experiences influences the overall way we feel. Many of us do not know that the way we see life is an implicit decision.

We know that reality is our experience of life. It is our veracity. We do not consider our perception as an acquired way of seeing things (often taken from our parents and our culture). They see that as being just the way things are. This fixed way of "the way things are" is called a "box," and our experience is that context in which we see the universe. And what we define as the truth is just how it feels.

But what if we could see a new way of looking at the truth? What if we could take the truth as we see it and hang it back on the wall in a new mental frame a broader, more open-minded frame? When we stared at that photo, we once again call it "the truth," how would we see that?

Only pretend you're in an art gallery. The image is hanging on the wall, and there is a guide pointing out to you its subtle details. You start noticing things you hadn't seen before. Before you see these new details were clearly there, but you missed them because you were too focused on what you thought was the most obvious theme. You decided it was a bad picture. The guy was the center, the woman was powerless, and the mood was bleak. You're about to move on, but now, with the help of the guide, you realize that there's a completely different line of the story to focus on in the picture. You see now that, behind the pair, there are jovial men bearing gifts entering in the room. A dog bit the man, which is why he looks mean and the woman is friendly and not powerless. The context you hadn't heard is a kid laughing, and the light coming through the glass is exceptional. There are many other things to focus on in the very same photo that you hadn't even seen. Experiencing this mental shift and experimentation, it feels exhilarating. The recollection of that image will be completely different now, and the way you express the thoughts with others about it will be likewise. Creating such alternate lines of stories with repetition becomes a talent, not a challenge. And in the future, you will be the reference that points out these alternative storylines.

4.2 Realistic Optimism

Would you believe that the opportunity to reframe a stressful situation a family question, a dispute with a coworker, a disobedient child like you did with this photo might actually change you are wellbeing? The response is a resounding yes! And for generations, it is something the Danes have been doing. They teach this invaluable skill to their children, and learning how to reframe early helps they grow up to be naturally better at it as adults. And being a reframe Master is a pillar of durability.

When it's snowy, rainy, and raining out, ask a Dane how he feels the weather is, and he will unintentionally answer: "Ok, it's a good thing I'm at work! "I'm happy I'm not on leave! "Tonight I'm looking forward to having a family at home." "There's no bad weather, just bad clothes! "In any subject, try to get a Dane to concentrate on something really bad, and you'll be mystified about how she can get a more positive outlook on the discussion.

"Yeah, but this is the last weekend of our lives!" And we don't mean to say the Danes have an overly positive outlook, using sugarcoat reframing of their lives. We don't float around on a bubble of hope frequently associated with super-happy people.

The "This is all so beautiful and perfect!" types," he said. Those who look like their eyes were stuck on and are still high on life. No, the Danes don't pretend there is no negativity. I just find out in a very matter-of-fact manner that there's also another aspect that you might never even have known of.

I choose to dwell of society on the positive, rather than on the negative. We shift their perspectives and reflect on the bigger picture instead of being stuck by one part of a debate, and we seem to be more balanced in their conclusions in general.

Danes are what psychologists call "realistic optimists." Realistic optimists with the glued-on eyes are different from those overly optimistic people those people who sometimes seem to be phone and life is so good. The problem of being excessively positive and optimistic is the same as at the opposite end of the spectrum, with the overly negative and depressive people. Very negative people tend to ignore positive information that can bring them down and make them unable to see a positive reality. On the other hand, overly positive people tend to ignore negative information, which can make them insensitive to significant negative realities. It's risky to force yourself to believe that it's all great, saying, "No, there's no problem at all," when it's really there. Underestimating negative situations can bring a much bigger blow when you're hit with one. It applies to the self-deception. It is much more in line with being a realistic optimist to be in touch with reality but to focus on the more positive angles.

Realistic optimists actually screen out needless negatives. We learn to tone down negative words and events and grow a pattern of viewing more objectively nuanced circumstances. They do not see what we think we feel.

Things just as bad or good or black or white, but realize instead that there are many shades in between. Focusing on circumstances with less negative aspects and seeking a middle ground reduces anxiety and increases well-being.

4.3 The expertise of Reframing

Most U.S. companies educate their staff in the ability to reinterpret or reframe details because it is seen as a key feature in resilience. Dean M. Becker, the founder of Adaptive Learning Systems, states in a Harvard Business Review article, "More than knowledge, more than practice, more than preparation, a person's level of endurance can decide who succeeds and who fails.

That is true in the cancer ward, in the Olympics and in the boardroom. "A key element to being successful is the ability to reframe negative situations.

Numerous studies indicate that when we consciously reinterpret an event to feel better about it, it decreases activity in areas of the brain involved in the production of negative emotions, and enhances activity in areas of the brain involved in cognitive control and adaptive integration. For one reframing study, images of angry faces were shown on two classes of participants. The first audience was advised to think that the people in the photos had just had a rough day and had nothing to do with their faces. The other party had been told to feel whatever feelings the faces elicited. What they discovered was that the group that had been taught to change their disposition toward the angry faces was not at all upset in reality, neural brain activity reported revealed that the reframing had washed out the unpleasant messages in their brain whereas the faces irritated the group that had been told to feel anything that had come to mind. Everything we think we feel.

Participants with phobias were introduced to spiders and snakes in a study done by academics at Stanford University. Each party had been educated to reframe their experience and not the other. The educated group displayed far less fear and panic than the control group and reported lasting changes in emotional responses when introduced to the spiders and snakes again later on. It shows the perceptual reframing's lasting impact.

Therefore, reframing not only affects our brain chemistry, but it also helps how we perceive pain, terror, anxiety, and the like. And this reframing relates directly to the words we use both clearly and in our ears.

The Limitations of Language

Limiting language has the opposite effect. Saying things like "I hate flying," "I'm terrible at cooking," or "I don't have willpower; that's why I'm so fat" is language limiting. "I just love flying once I get off the plane," "I like to use recipes while I cook," and "I'm trying to eat better and exercise more now" offer entirely different ways of looking at the same things. It's less black and white and less restrictive, and it has an entirely different feel. You see, our language is a choice, and it's crucial because it forms the framework we see the world through. We are also changing the way we behave by reframing what we mean into something more positive and less punishing.

It's unclear where the Danish inclination to reframe stems from. Realistic optimism appears to be just the default setting in Denmark; these reframing-related language choices are passed down through generations. Many Danes don't know they have that gift it's so much a part of how they are. And we are convinced that it is one of the reasons why Danes are so pleased to be voted on all the time.

4.4 How Reframing Works with Children

Reframing with children is about helping the child change the attention from what it feels it cannot do to what it can do. The parent lets the child view things from different angles, which allows the child to reflect on the less negative results or assumptions. This can become a default setting with practice- for both parent and child.

When you use restrictive words like "I hate this," "I can't do it," "I'm not good at that," and so on, you create a negative storyline. The storyline may have persuaded us that we are not good at anything, or that we are doing all wrong.

A kid who is told to restrict myths on "how he is" or how he should do something or handle things in different circumstances, he starts building coping strategies based on a lack of trust in his own ability in the face of new obstacles. "In athletics, she's not very good;" "He's too messy;" "She's so emotional." All of these are quite distinguishing. The more children learn of these claims; the more misleading assumptions they draw for themselves.

This lets your kids find and create a different story to raising the issue. We are encouraged to reframe by bringing them to a different, deeper, or vaguer view about themselves and the world around them. And this skill will transfer to the way in which they learn to see and interpret life, as well as others.

She reflects a great deal on reframing in Joseph's work as a narrative psychotherapist and, even more profoundly, on "authoring." She helps people look at the expectations they hold about themselves and the perceptions they place on their children without knowing it. Statements like "He's antisocial," "She's not very smart," "He's terrible at math," and "She's too vain" all become habits with which the kids try to make sense and relate. Families can hear kids say these things much more often than you know. Soon, they believe it has to be the way they are. You don't even try to make sense of it when new behavior doesn't fall into this category because they've already described themselves as being uncoordinated, shy, or bad at math.

The language we are using is extremely potent. It is the lens we view and identify ourselves and our world-image into. Allan Holmgren, a renowned Danish psychologist, argues that the vocabulary we use determines our reality. Any transition entails a language change. A problem is only a problem when it's considered a question.

The Influence of Labels

You know, many of these brands and stories bring us into adulthood. So much of what we think of ourselves as adults comes from the labels we were given as kids lazy, emotional, arrogant, dumb, and intellectual. Think about it: What are your beliefs about who you are, and how many of them come from what you were taught as a child? For the rest of our lives, many of us continue to live up to and unintentionally equate ourselves with those names. In breaking away from these stereotypes, we are opening new avenues of transformation for ourselves and our children.

Consider how common it is these days to hear people talking about children with disorders, even though they have never even seen a psychologist. It seems as though labelling babies, our own and others' as having psychological problems, has become completely natural. Shyness is named Asperger's, kids with a lot of energy are considered ADHD, kids who don't always grin must have depression symptoms, and the new thing we heard was a silent girl described as having sensory processing disorder. The parents were worried, the daughter was worried, and it was worrying to think that labelling her like that, without a diagnosis or a doctor's appointment, could have had an impact on her for the rest of her life.

It is very disturbing to say so nonchalantly that children suffer from a psychiatric or medical condition as if they are starving or cold. It not only ignores the extent and seriousness of those who are actually suffering from these disorders but it also wrongly marks them. Once they encounter a repetitive plotline in their lives, they continue to identify with those terms and draw conclusions about their identities from them. Such myths are becoming their story of life, and it is very difficult to get out of them. So by saying them, and then repeating them, we promote the very things we don't like in ourselves or in our children.

Through reframing, or authoring, we will continue to reinvent the future of our own and of our children.

Joseph shares an explanation of how she supports re-authoring in her work for adults and children. When someone comes to her who is unhappy with the way his life goes, she tries to talk about the things about himself that he is saying. She will discuss his negative conclusions on identity with him and try to separate him from those labels. One of her parents, for example, said she was idle and distracted and ruined her life. Then Joseph told her what this mark evoked and what sorts of emotions. The woman said it made her feel bad, particularly if she late forgets something or gets lost or sleeps. Those actions only made the bad mood deeper. Feeling sluggish made her feel as if she had lost, and she had no willpower. Therefore, once she said, "I am idle and distracted," she unintentionally repeated this plotline to others in her mind, and made it more prominent in her existence.

Joseph then used the language of externalization or language which separates the individual from the question. Laziness is not something in the genes; instead, it can influence people in different ways. Separating the individual from the issue makes us feel more capable of being active agents in our own lives to combat the crisis.

Joseph tried to help the customer imagine and explain laziness. Is that an unknown cloud? Is that just stifling you? What is it that makes you feel when it comes up? The woman said that it was like watching someone hold her down. It was hot air on top of her, and she was paralyzed; the alarm could not be turned off. As she attempted to read a map, it was foggy. If she wanted to exercise, it held her down. It made her feel weak, incompetent, and helpless.

We then went on to think about the feelings of laziness contrary. She spoke of what she cherished inside herself. She thought about what she wanted her future to be if she was able to shake off the heavy air that came upon her.

She then drew on past experiences and told another narrative about her life. It turns out she had outstanding communication skills and imagination. She was a funny friend and profoundly loyal. She was very talented in cooking and singing and had plenty of observations to choose from which she was not at all idle. She and Joseph have spoken about those encounters at length. So instead of concentrating on the negative character assumption of being weak and distracted, they focused on the ideals and talents of her story that they needed to "thicken." The more they focused on learning about the ideals and qualities she enjoyed about herself, the more the storyline about herself was optimistic and affectionate. Slowly, it began describing itself in a new way.

She was now imaginative, strong, and trustworthy, and found that she had the resources to reframe her outlook on her life and assumptions on her identity even more. Their outer voice was her inner voice of instruction. The problem was just the problem now; it was no longer who she was and it seemed impossible she would ever describe herself again as weak and dispersed. The strength of that vocabulary that characterized it was so much stronger than she ever knew.

Therefore, reframing or authorship is not about removing negative events in our life, but about putting less emphasis on these incidents and concentrating more on the aspects that we like. Just as in the painting from the beginning of the chapter: we can see a larger picture and practice concentrating on other aspects that tell a different story by being open to changing the background. We can transform our entire life experience into something better exactly the same for children. As adults, we are the guides to point out to them also a more positive and loving storyline.

How to Limit Language

Saying things like "She's such a picky eater," "He hates reading" or

"He's never listening" causes that behavior to define who kids are. The truth is, there is an emotion or attitude behind every action. It's still not set. We may be sick of something, or thirsty, or angry. The more that we can distinguish the behavior from the child, the more that we can change the way we see her and hence the way she sees her. It lets her know she is OK, and the action is not her destiny. As we have seen, labels can become a prophecy which fulfils itself.

Sometimes a stubborn kid may be very hard but try to see the bigger picture and what contributed to that action. Instead of saying how impossible the child is, and making him a problem, try to notice the story's other sides.

The kid who refuses to eat maybe had a snack before dinner and isn't really that hungry. The child who won't get dressed maybe is at the boundary-pushing age and doesn't understand why socks are important. And what more, are the other sides of this stubborn behavior? The kid may be very diligent and aggressive and show great leadership skills. Persistence is an important attribute that moves us far in life. Perhaps the disturbed kid is very artistic and enjoys painting. In exploring and encouraging the positive aspects of the undesirable activity, we can help our child concentrate on the better storyline. This also avoids other fights for authority and leads to happy parents and children.

4.5 The Danish Way of Reframing

All in all, Danes use less formal words and do not tell children what they believe or what they should do in different situations. You don't hear many adult thoughts about babies. "You ought not to be this way."

"Don't weep." "You ought to be very good! "He's mean! He's mean! "That's not how he should be." "You ought to remind him next time! "They tend to focus more on the use of the vocabulary that helps children understand why they feel and act. Of starters, if they are angry or upset, they try to help a child to understand why it is like this rather than how it should or should not feel.

"What is wrong? What is wrong? "Nothing." "It looks like it is wrong is it there?" Hey." "What is happening? "I don't remember." "You're sad? Angry? Angry? Happy? Happy? "I'm sorry." "Why do you feel sorry? "I'm sorry that Gary took my doll at playtime." Why do you think your doll was taken? "Because he's mean." "Is he mean; you think? Is Gary ever mean? "Yeah." "But you said you were playing a lot with Gary last week, right?"Yeah." "So what does it mean? "No." "Alright, Gary is good sometimes? "Yes." Yes. Danish parents help their children conceptualize their feelings and then guide them to something more positive rather than a disdainful or restricted view. It's the core of reframing.

"So what happened when the doll was taken? "I screamed." "I was so sorry that he took your baby. I can understand that. I can understand that. What do you think you can do if Gary takes your doll next time so that you won't be sad? "I can tell him to return it. Or I can say to his counsellor." "I guess it sounds like a good idea to advise him to give it back. Was Gary interested in playing with dolls? "Yes." "Is anything else that you can do but inquire it back? "We can play with the toys." "It sounds like a great idea. We know that Gary is actually a sweet boy, so you can ask next time if he too wants to play dolls. "Yes! "The lighter side of things can be seen with all sorts of situations, not just men. It is much easier to search a scene with experience to locate the hidden details that turn a scene into something positive. It can even be fun.

When an infant finds a better line in memory, try to replicate it, so it lasts. But ultimately, the solution should come from the child. It develops true self-esteem by becoming the master of her own internal responses. She doesn't know how to feel and act.

When we hold to the good in people and isolate acts from the individual, we teach our children that when they misbehave, we forgive them. Imagine if we said Gary's acts were stupid and evil. Children ' going to remember that. When it comes to our own children every time, they know why we judge. If we trust others and know how to forgive, we teach our children that when they misbehave, we forgive them. When we believe it is natural to lose because, given the fact we can see more positive things, our children will also be more compassionate when they fail.

Humor is another means of reframing. If you're on the side of a football field and your kid has played bad and says," I've done terribly',' a common way to respond is," No, you haven't. You played great! You played great! The camp was slippery! Each time you're going to win! You're winning some, and you're losing some!

"There may be a Scandinavian way of reframing with humor:" I played awfully." "Did you break your leg? "No, but I'm an awful player." "But didn't you break your leg, didn't you? Are you sure? Are you sure?"

(Go down to check the hip) Ok, you haven't break your leg, at least! "Ha-ha, I'm bad at soccer. I ought to stop. "You hate it? I hate it." Yeah, today you played pretty poorly, but remember that you scored two goals last week? "

All right, but. "Remember when you scored these goals, how did you feel? "Pretty good." "I think I remember you dancing and singing around the room.

How hate you, soccer? "No." "Precisely. Remember how you felt last week, and let's talk about what we can do to make you play better next week." "Practice again, I suppose." "Yeah, and let's go have some pizza and compliment you've never hurt your hip. "Some days are bad; some are fine." Note that the parent does not overlook the fact that the child was playing badly in this case. The adult understands, however, uses satire to demonstrate how much worse the situation could be and to direct the kid to positive feelings about playing football the previous week. That's a realistic optimist. You recognize reality, but you still can remove the needless negative words and focus on positive, not bad, emotions by laughter or another moment of good feeling. You give him the tools to deal with his singularity if you choose to tap into the positive aspects of any child's behavior. Everything is in the way you frame it. And realistic experience makes it perfect!

4.6 Tips for Reframing

- Take care of your negative behavior when you have a pessimistic habit of thinking. Only check to see how often you use fear to see a scenario. Try to find new ways of looking at stuff like doubts or problems that bother you as an exercise. Try to step back into perspective and see whether you are able to find a way of seeing it or a way of thinking on a more positive aspect.

- Talk about how rational the ideas are and try to change the world. Take the following phrases: "I never have time to practice. "I'm a terrible writer" "My baby's so irritating." Try to turn them into another paragraph. "More or less once a week, I attempt to practice, and I try eating lunch salads that look good." "I'm a pretty decent author once I'm into the field." "I love my mother-in-law, even if our differences are significant. She is a great grandmother for the children. "It can be difficult to do, but we know it makes a difference in our brain chemistry. It can even feel dumb at first, but the more you reframe, the better you feel. All we think and say bad about ourselves, our families and our anxieties and worries transmit directly to our children, so allow yourself and your children the blessing of retraining and helping them deal with the ups and downs of life.

- Use less restrictive words. Try to eliminate black and white, oppressive terminology. I love it, I always, I never, I never should, I shouldn't, I'm like that and so on. Limiting speech leaves little room for flexibility and only sees things from a different viewpoint. Seek to use less tense words. Use less judgment and tolerance, and your children and your wife will face fewer power struggles.

- Use the philosophy of externalization: isolate the behavior from the individual Rather than say "She is lazy" or "He is an aggressive person," use to see these issues as external rather than inherent. "It's laziness that is influenced by it," and "Moments of violence reaching him" are quite different from "how they are." 5. 5. Delete the story of your child for more love Make a list of the most negative qualities and actions of your child and write them down as a word. "I don't think he's got ADHD." "She's too persistent." And start editing the sentences to identify the source of these conducts. For instance, a person who is not very academic may like to read and be extremely social. The person with ADHD can be a strong and talented drummer. The stubborn man may be a hard-working patient who does not give up. Seek to focus on the positive side of the actions of your children, and they feel valued for their individuality rather than harshly identified. Rewrite your and your children's negative identification assumptions and isolate your actions from the boy. It encourages all parents and children to develop and compose their own love stories.

- Using language support Help your children by using language support rather than language constraint. Ask questions to help them identify their feelings. Enable them to recognize other people's intentions and actions so they can learn how to recover from difficult situations.

- Using comedy, listen to your kid and add fun to the situation to help transform things in a new way. Nevertheless, beware of not negating the thoughts or experience of the child.

Chapter 5: Empathy

5.1 E Is for Empathy

Maria and her sister had a very strained relationship for many years. Together usually involves lots of rolling eyes and uncomfortable thoughts. Frankly, they didn't like each other so much. Maria thought her sister was overwhelming with her parents ' experience as children, and her sister thought Maria was spoiled and insensitive. Both of those views made them territorial and distrustful of the other, leading to friction, disputes and increasing alienation with little expectation that their strong connection would ever be restored.

Not until Maria saw the friendship of her husband with his brother did she wonder if there was perhaps a better way. The two Danish brothers had as many disagreements and issues as the two American sisters, but Maria's husband treated them always with empathy and compassion rather than eyes and exasperation and, despite their differences, had a good relationship. So one day, Maria tried to listen, without her preconceived filters. She wanted to really explain how her sister felt and how upset she was. And what she found was that the role she had played was a remarkable change when she met her sister like a friend, not as a bitter rival.

Finally, Maria really saw the face of her sister. So she started to feel true sympathy for her, so vice versa. We spoke to each other as real caring friends for the first time in their lives. In a year the friendship improved dramatically, and now it has become unbelievably close. Where once she felt they were destined to divorce, Maria is now like a sibling would rely on her, and she is thankful for her life. It is a positive sea change, triggered by love together.

It's amazing how many people don't know the meaning of the word empathy. "Is that like friendliness? Apathy? Apathy? Homoeopathy? Homoeopathy? What is empathy, exactly? "If so few people know what empathy means, how many people incorporate it into their day-to-day life, what is really surprising about this confusion? Empathy is the ability to understand and acknowledge others ' emotions. It's capable of feeling what someone else feels not just caring with them, but also connecting for them. Simply put, it runs a mile in the shoes of someone else. So saying is much better than doing. Why is it so hard? Has it anything to do with our culture?

A recent study showed that empathy for young people in the US had fallen almost 50% since the 1980s and 1990s. In the meantime, the narcissism degree has doubled. Narcissism is an abused image of the self that seeks to isolate the self and discourage meaningful relationships. The attributes of narcissists are such that people rely so much on themselves that they are losing attention to the interests of others. There are many reasons that this may be so, but no one seems entirely aware of why.

The Narcissistic Personality Indicator (NPI) was created in 1970 to measure narcissism, and a large number of tests have shown its validity. Jean Twenge and her associates examined NPI values for college students between 1982 and 2007 and found that narcissism increased significantly and consistently during that twenty-five-year period. The degree rose so drastically that almost 70 per cent of college students were arrogant higher than the average college student in 1982 by 2007. What might be the explanation for this?

The Heart of America: Survival of the Fittest

In the United States, individuals by humans have been considered to be fundamentally selfish, violent and competitive for many years. This began with the industrial revolution.

At least partially, the structure of the market economy and of the financial, legal and political systems is based on this concept, which essentially opposes each other. The message of covetousness on Wall Street is just one indication of this lack of empathy. For so many a year, evolutionary theorists, politicians and the general public have reflected on rivalry and on the imprudence of natural selection as the way people are drawn. Ayn Rand, whose philosophy many people admire, supports the belief that the human being is inherently egotistical and that the human being is here for his own sake. If you believe in this idea or not, the fact is that these ideas are so deeply rooted in American culture that most people don't know it. This penetrates daily life. Competition and desire to be number one are part of what Americans think.

Let's talk about the mothers you knew for a moment. How many really open up and share what happens to their children? How many are courageous enough to be honest and don't know if they're doing the right things? Currently, it seems that fewer moms are able to demonstrate their insecurity as the scope of what it means to be a "healthy" mother has gradually been applied to expectations which are able to live up to and even compare with other mothers. If you feed your child (breast milk, organic, healthy, etc.) or offspring events (how many they participate in and how good they are) or schooling, in what should be a simple everyday interaction, there's often a feeling of one-way. Naturally, this sense of increasing competition is not limited to childcare. It permeates all manner of expressions. It can be very discreet, but you might be shocked if you pay attention, how often you find it is just under the surface.

Many people are afraid that they are really open and vulnerable because they don't want to be judged or rejected. And many relationships are reduced to superficialities in this terror.

Our Fear of Vulnerability and the Discovery of the Social Brain

Brené Brown, a popular risk expert, says that people are scared of being vulnerable because they are actually afraid of being isolated. We want social connections so much that we are afraid to say something that someone else can reject us. Yet being weak and empathic helps to bring us closer. So we are switching from insecurity to the other side of the spectrum. Instead of attempting to use empathy and understand why a person chooses (to breast-feed, to work or not to work, to name only a few of the big ones), we regret her. "How can she work with foreigners and leave her child? I could never do that! I could never do that! "What can a housewife be like? I could never do that! I could never do that! "How long will she breast-feed? It is gross! It is filthy! "How couldn't she breast-feed? It's so egotistical! "And so it starts. The broad brush of judgment is swiped over another human. You're equal to all of your decisions, so naturally, you're a better parent. Because the highest is a commodity, we greatly admire. The cruel irony is that we would be much abler to feel encouraged, not manipulated by a linked social network.

The issue with guilt and always trying to be different is that we become extremely uncomfortable or nervous as we encounter our own feelings of insecurity. And what do people do when they experience some kind of fear or discomfort?

The most common reaction is to get stomached. Meat, Television, shopping, food, medicine and drink are all good treatments to stuff and feel all right at that moment. But it's just a band-help.

Nonetheless, everybody seems to have at their hands a box of these Band-Aids. Brown says in her TED address on poverty: "We are the most vulnerable society in the world, bloated, overweight and sick."

That makes us wonder: what if we sought a little more compassion and kindness rather than punishing others? What if we stop trying to achieve perfection which does not exist? What if we were trying to connect more?

Pioneering neuroscience research has shown what scientists call the' inner brain,' a brain region that lights up when we engage in social activities. Matthew Lieberman, a social cognitive neuroscientist, wrote: "This network is a reflection that enables us to think about the mind, thoughts, feelings and goals of other people. This encourages understanding and empathy, solidarity and compassion. "Lieberman is of the view that we are not only linked to self-interest, but also to other people's welfare.

The Surprise of the Dilemma of Prisoners

Lieberman set up a neuroimaging study with functional magnetic resonance imaging (fMRI), which examines human blood flow to various parts of the brain, to test human beings, while psychologically testing them called the "dilemma of a prisoner" How much each person gets depends on whether or not the other person splits things fairly. If both players decide to cooperate, then each player receives $5. If one works together, the other "defects" the cooperative player doesn't get anything, and the defector gets all 10 dollars. Each one gets one dollar if both defects. The challenge is to determine what you should do without understanding the opinion of your mate. It's safer to defect: you're going to get at least one dollar and perhaps ten. When you cooperate, if your friend loses, you lose nothing.

The findings showed that the players decided to collaborate more than allowing the selfish choice of injuries, contrary to what the researchers predicted.

However, the findings of fMRI show that activation in the ventral striatum (primary reward area for the brain) decreased as long as both participants interacted. And this award center was more prone to the total amount of both players than to one's own personal performances. This means that people have more satisfaction than their own joy from the happiness of others! What might this explain? The Danes have always had an underlying conviction that caring for the welfare of other people is important for their own happiness, and they judge on something by these scientific findings!

5.2 The Truth about Empathy

Empathy was historically considered to separate people from animals. Most thought that animals and primates showed no empathy. But in his book The Age of Empathy, the renowned primatologist Frans de Waal reveals that empathy is indeed evident in all kinds of animals. Research shows affection for rodents, priests, monkeys, dolphins, elephants and other species, but the general public learns little about them. This is because so many of our governing policies were founded on the conviction that nature is a "life fight" and that our societies should be built on competition and selfishness, not on the full spectrum of what it means to be human.

Empathy is a beneficial instinct from an evolutionary point of view, which helps us live in communities. Without empathy and solidarity, humans could not have survived. Unlike popular belief, most of us are concerned with the well-being of others. This impulse was just asleep because of lack of focus.

People thought babies were born without empathy. But that's just not true. We all have to be wired for empathy; just know how to link the wires and make them work.

Empathy resides in the limbic system of the brain. Memory, feelings and instinct are regulated. It is a fluid neural network of mirror neurons and insula. How many don't know is that we are physically susceptible to communicating with others. This is made possible by a large number of neuronal systems embedded in the right hemisphere of the brain, which is important to the mirror neurons.

You see, the self is not an independent person, but a connected structure.

"Empathy is not a privilege for people, and it is a need," Daniel Siegel, UCLA's clinical professor of psychology says. We're not living because we have claws and we don't have large fangs. We exist because we can connect and work together. "Empathy makes our relationship with others better. During infancy, it grows through the connection to the attachment figure. A kid first learns to respond to the feelings and moods of his parents and then to other men.

The infant should feel and imitate what the mother feels. This is why issues like eye contact, facial expressions and voice tone are so critical at the start of life. This is the first way we feel trust and connection and start to learn empathy.

For a fact, when the kids hear them cry, they often soothe other babies with pacifiers or a fuzzy animal. They respond by being frightened or afraid to cry from others, and some even start crying when they hear it. You may not understand why or the feeling behind this weeping, but you will know with time and experience.

Studies show that children aged eighteen months almost always try to help an adult who visibly struggles with a task. If the adult is asking for anything, the kid tries to give it to him, or if the child sees the parent slip, it picks it up.

On the other hand, if the same person drops it firmly to the table, the kid will not pick it up for him. She realizes it was intentional, and the adult doesn't want it. Even before children are taught to support or to be careful maybe before they realize that it is a duty they are less greedy than is often believed.

5.3 The Responsibility of Parents

Parents have a huge responsibility because they are the main example of empathy and have to be empathic. This can be achieved by using their vocabulary and actions. Children are continually focused on and mirroring their kin. Therefore, what you feel in your home is essential to your empathy.

The families in which children are exposed to physical, psychological or sexual abuse are the kinds of families which can quash their ability to empathize. Their healthy boundaries and their ability to feel for others are broken. Every child suffering from an attachment disorder is impaired by its empathy ability.

Other types of family that can affect the development of a child's empathy are overprotective. These are the parents who fear failure or the great emotion of their children and who do whatever they can to prevent conflict and fulfil all their children's wishes. Sometimes these parents conceal their logical, irrational and emotional reactions to "protect" their children. This hinders the children's ability to read their own feelings, which, in effect, will reduce their ability to empathize (because what they see and hear is not what parents confirm). Often, children from overprotective families are more susceptible to narcissism, anxiety and depression. You cannot self-regulate because of the difference between thought and behavior.

Kids that are consistently told how to act and behave will not grow into individuals that are respected and allowed to display their full range of emotions. We may be detached from how we feel, which makes it difficult to navigate the many decisions in life safely. You can experience persistent vacuity and frustration. What can we say when we don't know how we feel?

Encouraging childhood sensitivity early on helps to build healthy relationships in the future. So we believe that these loving relationships are the root of true happiness and well-being.

How Do the Danes Learn to Be So Empathic?

In the Danish school system, the nationwide standardized curriculum Step by Step was already introduced as a pre-school. Each child's pictures show different emotions: depression, terror, rage, disappointment, joy, etc. Kids speak about these cards and bring in words what the infant feels and tries to conceptualize the thoughts of one's own and others. We learn empathy, solve problems, monitor themselves and interpret facial expressions. An important part of the program is that facilitators and children do not evaluate their feelings. Instead, they just recognize and respect them.

CAT-kit is another system which is becoming more and more popular. The curriculum aims to enhance emotional awareness and understanding and reflects on how perceptions, thoughts, emotions and senses are communicated. Resources in the CAT kit include picture markers, emotionally-intensive measuring sticks and images of the body, in which participants are able to draw the physical and emotional dimensions. There's also a tool called My Circle, in which children draw their peers, family members, experts and outsiders to help them understand others.

The Mary Foundation has also greatly influenced empathy training in schools. Mary, the Crown Princess and the forthcoming Queen of Denmark have developed a country-wide anti-bullying program. Free of Bullying is a program where young people between three and eight talk about bullying and teasing so that they can learn to be more concerned about each other. It has produced positive results, which are recommended to other institutions by more than 98% of teachers.

Another less obvious example of Danish school empathy is how they combine children of different strengths and weaknesses. Students who are academically stronger are taught together with less strong children; shier children with gregarious children; and so on. This is quietly handled. The teacher gets to know the students over time and then sits them. The aim is to make sure that everyone has positive qualities and to help each other reach the next level. The math whiz may be bad in football, and vice versa. This system promotes collaboration, coordination and loyalty.

Studies show that in teaching others, there is an enormous learning curve. Students who instruct others have more difficulty understanding, remember and use the content more accurately. However, they must also try to understand other students ' perspectives to help them where they find themselves in trouble. The ability to explain complex topics to another student is not an easy task, but an invaluable ability to live.

And as Joseph observed in her teaching years, this kind of teamwork and sensitivity always gives children a strong degree of satisfaction and joy. It returns to the collective brain, and the problem of the inmate is what we saw at the fMRI. In reality, contrary to what we might believe, people's minds are more pleased that they partner than compete alone.

So it may not be shocking that empathy is one of the most important factors for successful managers, businessmen, administrators and businesses. This decreases abuse, increases our empathy and significantly improves partnerships and social connections. Empathy improves the quality of meaningful relationships, one of the most important factors in our sense of well-being, we learn. Empathetic teens are more successful because they are motivated by a greater purpose than their cynical peers. And it makes sense if you think about it. Successful people do not work alone; we each need the help of others to produce positive results in our lives.

Perhaps by concentrating on consciously teaching our children empathy as they do in Denmark, we will make our adults happy in the future.

5.4 The Power of Word

The prominent Danish philosopher and theologian Knud Ejler Løgstrup claims parents can nourish the minds of their children more than merely through amusement and language translation. We should also cultivate their empathy. He said that words or stories that we tell about others are essential in order to teach our kids how to put themselves in another's shoes.

Of starters, when Danes speak to their own children about other children, it is pretty extraordinary to hear the words they use. We don't talk about them consciously. These are essential words used by all parents when referring to others. They are phrases. Yet their propensity to point out the good character of other children is strong.

"He's such a sweet boy, isn't he?" is very common to hear "She's very kind, don't you believe that? "It's been very effective, haven't you thought so?

"He's good. You think so? You think so? "What makes it amazing is to think about how these word choices lay the groundwork for the positive of others as a potential norm. It is normal to see the positive in others by pointing out the good in others. Trust becomes more normal. Nevertheless, it is unusual for a Danish adult to talk critically about another child before their own.

Alternatively, they try to explain others ' actions and why they might have behaved disagreeably. "She was definitely really sleepy and missing her nap." "Did you think he was starving? We try to lead the children to think that a child's behavior is simply influenced by a situation instead of portraying the child as cruel, egotistical or strange.

This is actually how the ability to reframe starts. Being able to imagine quickly that someone might have trouble allows us to see his or her actions plainly. Instead of swiping a wide brush with a negative label, we should empathize. That also makes us feel better because it saves a lot of money. Otherwise, negative energy would be lost.

Løgstrup wasn't naive to believe that trusting others was necessarily rewarded. He simply believed that trust is a fundamental element of being people, like other "supreme manifestations of creation," such as speech honesty, love and compassion. "To show faith and confidence in others is to give oneself." And this is valid. Confidence is very easy.

The Danish Way of Teaching Empathy

One of the first things to consider when it comes to teaching empathy is to differentiate between the capacity for empathy and the consequences that is, how one should bring empathy into motion in relation to others. This needs to be learned, and many good examples from parents and others with children on a daily basis take a long time.

Just give us an example. Lisa plays with a shovel along the sea, and Mark, a little boy, wants to play with it, but Lisa doesn't want it. Mark starts crying. Mark starts crying. What is she going to do? What many people would do is give Mark the shovel as he cries. But what does this teach? What does it teach? Is it real that we always have to give others what they want just because they want it? Again, this is teaching how to do things because there is an extrinsic effect rather than an inner rationalization. Lisa works with the shovel and can tell that Mark gets upset. She needs an adult to help her balance her own needs and limitations and then to decide for herself and take responsibility for herself. What often occurs in such conflicts is that the adults have mercy on Mark and demand that Lisa carry out the compassion of the adult and force him to give Mark the shovel. It's not rational or empathetic. This does not mean that Lisa should not try to consider the feelings of other people not at all but it is also important to educate children that adults have empathy and sympathy for them, and to realize how they feel and what their desires are so that they can really appreciate them themselves. It also tells Mark that by crying, he does not actually do anything.

So what can the father of Lisa do? After the children let themselves find a solution, Lisa's mother or dad could read their body language and ask if she would like to share it. The parent may propose a plan Lisa spends another five minutes with the toy, and then Mark can borrow it while Lisa starts a new project. It's fun to chat and play together if you're in a mood for it. It's all right to say no at times, but it's also important to learn how to share and appreciate it.

In the long run, these exercises over sensitivity can be immense.

It becomes a powerful lesson in the long run as you teach a child not to be compelled to do something purely through appeasing another or making things simpler.

Teenagers subject to the wrong kind of peer pressure will easily stand up to what they think is right because their thoughts have been shown to be legitimate from the very beginning. When we educate our children with empathy, they can appreciate and apply it themselves even better. If your inner compass is good, it leads you in the right direction.

One way Danish parents encourage empathy is by pointing out the feelings of other people to their children. It's not unusual to hear stuff like this: "Aw, you can see that Victor cries? Why do you think he's weeping? "She looks angry. Why do you think she's furious? "You're angry, I can see. Can you try to explain why to me? "It's very rare to hear anyone say,' don't be like that. "Why is she mad? There's no need to be upset." That's absurd! "You don't have anything to cry stop crying! "Why are you so angry?!"You ought to be satisfied! "Do Danish parents tend to understand the feeling when talking to the kid at leastoh? Why are you crying? Why are you crying? "And they sit down to show them they're seeing them.

"You're mad, I see. What's worried about you? How did she take your toy? She's only a small baby. I don't believe she did so intentionally, do you? "There are not always good reasons for or easy solutions for a child's emotions, but we teach respect, at least by admitting them and not trying to judge them. Imagine if adult mental issues were constantly ignored as irrational, inappropriate or wrong and instead it asked us how to act.

One of the foundations of understanding in Danish is not judgment. The Danes try not to judge too harshly their children, friends, friends of their children or family. Both family members have the right to be heard and taken seriously, not just the one who yells loudly. It is important to be respectful of yourself and others.

So note that you will help your kids grow up to be less judgmental in the long term by fostering a more empathetic, less bullying so insecure, honest attitude in your family including yourself.

5.5 Tips for Empathy

- Understand your own empathic style. There are questions that you have to think and speak about: what is empathy for me? To my wife, what does empathy mean? Where are we in agreement and disagreement? What are our core values? How do I judge myself and others? How do you judge my other partner? How does this reflect our language style? How can I change my language style to a more empathetic and less judgmental style? Remember, this isn't easy, but you'll get better with practice. Seek first to listen to yourself and see what you're thinking about and then learn of different ways to express yourself with more sensitivity. Remember, your kids are reflecting you. Help your partner to do the same thing.

- Understand others to understand other people rather than to shame them. You'll be surprised how often you judge others and how much it takes to find a reason to defend them by putting yourself in their shoes. This is really a form of empathy.

- Notice and try to identify emotions. Help your child see the emotions of others and experience one's own without making a judgment. "Was Sally angry? Why was she furious? What happened? What happened? What do you think of what happened? What do you think? "Not' she ought not to be angry and have done it.' Read, read, read studies show that children's reading significantly increases their empathy. And reading books that cover all emotions, including negative and uncomfortable ones, not only good books. Dealing with reality, even at the level of infants, is truthful and genuine and has proved to boost sensitivity dramatically.

- Improve meaningful relationships Try to patch your own relationships with empathy. It has been shown that broken relationships cause physical and psychological damage. Empathy and compassion stimulate the same brain region, making it easier for you to forgive and be forgiven; the more your empathy skills are improved. Meaningful friendly relationships and family relationships are the main factors determining true happiness, far beyond money.

- Try to be more vulnerable and don't be afraid to be vulnerable. It's what we can do most connecting. Learn, be interested, think and use metaphors to respond carefully.

- Seek empathy in others, encourage friends and family who want to cultivate empathy and kindness. New mothers and parents can greatly benefit from this support.

Chapter 6: No Ultimatums

6.1 N Is for No Ultimatums

We were all there. We're tired, our children disobey or not listen and, despite all our efforts, they're still misbehaving or annoying, and we're snapping. Many adults shout and scream, many people threaten to take time out, and some use physicality.

We saw many friends and fellow parents shouting or spreading their babies. It often comes from a child's anger that doesn't listen to an ultimatum. Normally the scene goes as follows: "You could do it better right now or else!" or" If you don't interrupt it now, you'll get it. Yes, I know it! I mean it! "When I ask you again, that's it! "And once the ultimatum is out and all options are expended, the parents feel that they have to go about it to gain control and the outcome results in some form of spanking, yelling or exercise.

Several studies suggest that up to 90% of Americans still use spanking on their children as a punishment. Like her twin, Maria was spanked as a child. Parents who usually spank only work from their own default settings based on their education, which is typically quite physical.

Maria has never been debating spanking as a form of punishment for many years. Just recently was teachers ' corporal punishment eliminated when she was in elementary school. She thought it was quite normal and never felt that she had a problem with it.

Only when she was pregnant with her first child did she realize how different her husband's perspective on discipline was from her own.

Her discussions on the topic and her increased understanding of the Danish upbringing of her husband prompted her to take another approach. Like so many aspects of understanding the Danish Way, the journey to this discovery opened the eyes.

As we read this book, we found that there are still nineteen states in the United States where physical punishment in schools is still permitted. This is to hit students with a paddle or a cane. Although corporal punishment is prohibited in schools in 31 states, it is still permitted in private schools in all 50 states. This may or may not surprise you. The point is: there is still a prevalence of spanking.

Nevertheless, a large-scale study carried out through parental methods in the United States by the Centers for Disease Control and Prevention (CDC) shows that we use physicality more than one could imagine. The study measured five cultural groups, consisting of 240 focus groups in six different cities (Asian, Hispanic, African American, Non-Hispanic Whites and American Indians), which found that all groups were claiming to be physically punished sometime or another.

The similarities between societies in terms of when and where the range was even more surprising. For examples, African American mothers said they spanked. On the other side, white and American Indian parents felt embarrassed in public. White parents often talked in a restaurant (which came up frequently during discussions) of taking the child into the bathroom to span the span, while Indian parents preferred to delay it until they got home. This just shows that behind closed doors, more spanking may occur.

6.2 Four Parenting Styles

Whether or not a parent uses a body sanction, social researchers categorize childhood styles into four distinct types.

Authoritarian: These parents are aggressive, not sensitive. They want obedience and high standards, the classic tiger mother. Authoritarian parents ' children tend to do well in school but sometimes experience poor self-esteem, depression and social skills.

Authoritative: These parents are authoritative and attentive (not to be confused with authoritarian). They also set high standards, but support their discipline. Authoritative parent children are more socially and intellectually competent than other parents.

Allowable: These parents are highly responsive but rarely need their child's behavior, based on their child's self-regulation. Kids of permissive parents tend to have academic issues and general behavior.

Uninvolved: These parents are not attentive or aggressive, but are not neglectful. Uninvolved parents ' children are the worst in all regions.

Authoritarian parents are characterized as poorly receptive and controlled. The abusive parents ' reaction to a child wondering why it would be "Because I've said that." Children are not expected to question why.

Authoritarian upbringing poses several problems. First of all, being highly controlled will make children revolt. Furthermore, not having any encouragement apart from' because I have said so," pull up your socks," straighten up,' and' it is my way or the lane' leaves children alone to control their feelings that can be both overwhelming and disturbing, combined with fear and shame.

Authoritarian parents usually behave this way because they have been raised and feel good. And perhaps they did. But if somebody claims that they smoked all their lives and were all right, does it mean that smoking is good for us?

The Hard Truth about Spanking

A recent analysis of two decades of research on the long-term effects of physical punishment on children found that spanking is not only not effective, but can also wreak havoc on children's long-term health.

The study found that not one of over 80 studies, regardless of the age and sample size of the children, has found a positive relationship with physical punishment. Not one. Not one. What correlations he noticed were these: spanked children can feel depressed and devalued. We can suffer from their sense of self-worth. High penalties can lead to backfiring, as they can encourage children to lie in desperate order to avoid being released. Physical punishment is associated with problems of mental health later in life, including depression, anxiety and use of drugs and alcohol. Neuroimagery reveals that physical punishment will change parts of the brain that are involved in IQ tests and increase the likelihood of substance abuse. And there are data showing that spanking can affect areas of the brain that control feelings and stress.

Parents are wobbling because they think it is successful. And perhaps it's, in the short term. But beyond that, it's quite ineffective. Children learn to listen because they're frightened. Power struggles build isolation and animosity rather than proximity and belief. Distance and animosity produce anger (or obedience, but with diminished self-esteem), opposition and revolt. And where do you go after you hit them if the bad behavior continues? Hit them more? Hit them harder?

Scream more laudable? Hit some more of them? It is not shocking that violence is one of the most common long-term effects of spanking.

Case in point: A woman in a spanking study conducted by a parenting specialist George Holden struck or kicked her baby after the bachelor: "It's to make you learn not to hit your mother. "And let's not mention how many of us adults practice this activity unconsciously. Yet do we ever ask the question, "Is it appropriate to yell or stretch incessantly? "Many of us don't ask that question until it's too late.

What are the best feelings of the universe about spanking, yelling, and power struggles?

Spanking became illegal in Denmark in 1997. The majority of Danes agree that using spanking as a form of discipline of an infant is extremely strange and almost incomprehensible. It was discontinued in Sweden earlier, in 1979. More than 30 nations now have similar laws, including most of Asia, Costa Rica, Israel, Tunisia and Kenya.

Across Denmark, the parenting style is very egalitarian. It is closely connected with the style of authority. This ensures that they create rules and guidelines to be practiced by their children. Nevertheless, they are very open to questions about the rules for their babies. Danes regard children as inherently good and therefore react to them. Of example, what we call the younger years is an interesting difference in language between Danish and English. In English it's called "the terrible twos," while in Danish it's called the "border age" trod alder; it's natural and pleasant, not disruptive and horrible children pushing boundaries. When you look at it like this, the abuse is better to accept than to see it as evil and deserving of retribution.

You rarely hear this in Denmark when you yell and scream at your children.

A household full of yelling is indeed an extremely rare occurrence. How do they do? How do they? One of the parents we met expressed it quite well: "First of all, I think that we should keep quiet as parents and try not to lose control. How can we trust our children to control themselves if we can't? This does not mean that the Danes are weak or soft not at all, but steadfastness and kindness can replace a loss of temper and immediate power struggles and ultimatums. Avoiding these creates a quieter and safer atmosphere.

Parenting with Respect

The Danes expect their children to be polite, but respect goes in both ways. You must send it in order to receive it. Governance with fear is a problem because it does not encourage respect; it encourages fear. There is a distinction between solidity and terror. With panic, the kid won't ever know why he shouldn't do anything. He just wants to avoid getting hurt or yelled at. This does not make a strong sense of self simpler. A strong meaning of the heart is the asking and comprehension of which laws and why, and then the integration and recognition of them. Fear of what is known as a statute is very special. Working in a violent, shouting atmosphere does not help. And likewise, if she is afraid of you, you won't know if her kid is honest with you in the future. Maybe she'll tell you what she thinks you want to hear out of fear. Fear is strong but not conducive to an atmosphere of proximity and confidence. If you foster an atmosphere of respect and peace in which there is no fear of guilt, shame, or pain, you will have a much more positive influence and a true closer relationship.

In reality, studies show that children from trustworthy parents are more likely to be self-reliant, socially accepted, productive academically and behavioral.

Depression and anxiety are less likely to be reported, and antisocial behavior such as delinquency or alcohol use is less common. Research suggests that even one powerful parent could make an enormous difference. Children are also better adapted to their parents and less affected by their peers. A study of American students showed students a number of moral problems and asked them how they would solve them. Students from leading families were more likely than others to say that their parents should influence their decisions rather than their peers.

6.3 How Danish Practice No Ultimatums at School

One way Danish schools promote democracy is to encourage students, together with their teacher, to set up rules each year. At the beginning of school, teachers talk to their students about what it means to have a good class and what their principles and actions are structured to make it a good class. The laws can be anything from time to time, including consideration for others. However, what is important is that everyone decides jointly on the code of conduct. No set of rules is the same for any gender. And they do this each year because the graduates are older and more mature than the previous years and have different senses of obligation.

The results are amazing. For starters, if somebody was too disruptive or interrupting, in her daughter Julie's class one year, the entire class had to stand up and walk around the room to clap her hands ten times. They both discussed this at the beginning of the year. Children who are too loud find like their classmates have direct responsibility and influence, not just on their teachers. This can be a surprisingly strong incentive to stop.

Within Denmark, they spend much more time and money talking about how problems can be solved rather than disciplined.

Most Danish schools are fitted with various types of equipment for students to deal with different problems. Of starters, kids with ADHD or hyperactivity will sit on a ball coil, allowing them to concentrate in class. This ball coil has spicy relaxation buttons on one leg. It activates the postural muscles so that the student sits more upright and retains equilibrium and improves concentration unconsciously.

Schools also include "fidget packs" and "cuddle things" for children who have trouble keeping still, which can lead to distractions for others. Such packages contain items like stress balls and spaghetti-like loops, which can be used to relax and concentrate them on. Children who are too noisy or violent may be asked to spend time on their own to help them consume some of the excess energy.

Danish teachers are also trained to follow the principle of differentiation. This essentially means teachers learn to see each student as a person with specific needs. They plan with each student and keep track of their growth twice a year. Academic, personal and social objectives can be achieved. The hope is that the instructor is better able to understand their individual needs by "differentiating" the students so they can respond and react accordingly.

This is crucial because, as we saw in previous chapters, it makes a big difference in your response to them that you choose to see them. You will react accordingly if you see them as nonsense and exploitation. When you consider them as innocent, you are much more likely to react by feeding them and by loving them, even by encouraging them than by punishing them. When one sees benevolent intentions and kindness in another annoying child, patience is much easier to mobilize. This is a loop that returns to you. Better begets better. Worse begets worse. Peace gives birth to peace. Recall, it's not the bad child, it's the bad behavior. This differentiation is always significant.

6.4 Avoiding Power Struggles

Joseph tells us of how, when she was teaching, she stopped power struggles with a classmate. There was a kid who was very offensive and defiant in her class. He got the "disorder makes" mark. Many of the students thought that Joseph was perhaps too straightforward with him, but she believed it was incredibly important to stay away from making him a poor boy and having a lot of confrontation. She knew that he had a rough house life, and she saw him always as a cute, caring child. He was funny and smart, so she concentrated on his qualities and chose to ignore the rest so as not to reinforce his bad story. She listened kindly to him and focused on his ability to be a good guy.

Several years later, despite bad feelings, the student came to a school gathering. He turned his life entirely around and came to say thank you. He recalled that Joseph wasn't worrying about him, so she knew that he would do well in life. He said that her confidence in him gave him the power to support himself and become a better person. Joseph was deeply touched. She then realized how important it really is to separate the behavior from the person. Trusting, encouraging and treating people as actions rather than as the individual, helps to create a more caring tale of life.

We have, therefore, now seen why a more inclusive approach directly enhances our children's well-being, joy and resilience. How can we not follow the Danish way of ultimatums?

Put a Mirror Up to Yourself

Think about the things that you do not like to hear about yourselves and then put up a mirror. That's what your child's going to get. If you don't like the shouting and the exasperating paws, don't do it. Don't do it if you don't like physicality.

Stop Thinking About What Others Think

Stop thinking about what others say about you or about the actions of your kids. Yelling and physicality are often overshadowed by someone who is watching you. Regardless of whether you are at the home or a friend's house, in a restaurant or store, keep your actions in accordance with your beliefs. It's about honesty and conformity with what you believe. Don't think about how others raise their children or how your family believes you should raise their children. Concentrate on doing what is best for your kids and trust in that success. Some parents only replicate behaviors of their own. In making a change, you are doing something even bigger and harder. Try to form a group of parents who communicate and support each other in the Danish Way. Believe in your beliefs and stand by your sacrifices. The data is in the test to make us happy, more resilient and better adjusted.

The Danish Way works. Don't go there if you feel torn about a power struggle to eat or polite or belligerent with friends or family. Breathe, just stay calm, and remember. You are using satire. Use humor. Offer a way out. Offer a way out. Don't think about how a friend could judge you or your children or not. Your offspring will be happier and healthier in the long run, which is what matters.

Chill Out and Remember the Big Lines

Know the difference between fighting and battle and don't fight. Does it really matter that your clothing or hair always look perfect? Is it really necessary that one day they don't wear the Batman shirt?

Do you really have to scrub your plate right now because you said so? Or are they trying to lettuce because they need to? Is it really valuable? It is what you and your friend must decode and determine whether broad lines are to be applied.

Maybe it's not the right time for a friend's house or a restaurant. What are your main lines, and when will you actually try to educate and enforce them? Ask yourself if it respects you and your child to make a scene public. You must be persistent, but you must not lift troops. Note, infants experience periods where they don't want to do/eat / wear / say those things. They emerge from them. They rise. When you follow the big lines, they will recognize them. The key is having patience and the courage to go through these periods without losing the coolness and concentrating on what is important.

Maria's father, for some time, refused to wear a sweater or shoes. It was exhausting, and nothing helped but to take it outside without a sweater or a scarf, and her daughter said, "Oh, I'm cold; I'll put that on! "It took a while, but she grew up. For a while, she didn't say hi to people either. People stopped and said hi, and she was looking away. Yet Maria never pushed it. Maria kept reminding her. She began to say hello one day, six months later, and from there on, she managed to do so.

Children are also checking things for themselves. If it becomes too much a power game, everyone loses, and life gets bad. If you're cool, they're cool.

Examples of No Ultimatums: Offering a Way Out

Typical answer: "Don't throw it! When you chuck it again, that's it! "Take it away. Take it away. Distract. Distract. Remove the child. Remove the child. You are using satire. Use humor. Stay cool about it when you say no. Tell the kid what it can do to chuck it. Mime to give it back an "ow-ow" from being struck by the rock. Show him again, shake your head and look distressed, if he throws it back. "Ow, ow, ow, ow! "The first time he may not be able to get it, but he will understand more and more over time.

It is wrong to beat or pinch someone, and you should be strict in those situations and hug the kid and tell them "No! "Forcibly. Let her smile at you and give you an apology and caress so that she knows the meaning of sadness and the lack of physicality at an early stage. Note, it needs to happen soon because children forget what they did immediately. You have to deal directly with this behavior. Children may not understand the meaning of grief at first, but they will become empathized with time and learning.

Dinnertime Often Means Power Struggles

How hungry a child responds to food? When, for example, he eats more in the day, he still isn't very hungry. Or he might be so hungry that he needs to regulate his blood sugar in order to feel better. Eating blood sugar controls the way a child functions. Empathy helps you understand from where he comes and reacts accordingly. Learning, instead of getting upset is a good starting point. Imagine how you'd feel if you were too hungry or over, either way and then leave there.

Something to remember: encouraging a kid to love and value food is an outstanding gift. Nutrition is what sustains us, and having a healthy, loving relationship will build a happy life. Check your own diet relationship and make sure it's as healthy as possible. Basically, meals should be a fun time for the family to come together.

Put a little of it all on the plates of your kids and allow them to eat the food they want. Food conditions will above all be nice and cozy, not tensioned and focused on children having to eat. Under these conditions, most people would lose their appetite!

If you do it a lot, it will be a lot.

There's milk.

They can come back for it if they want it. We don't always love food, we don't always scrub our dishes, or we don't want to

try things that we don't.

Occasionally we do, but not always. Give kids a way out if you can. You will be more valued when you find a guideline for yourself. Bear in mind also that you are the source.

Low stress uncharged everything, particularly nourishment. Remember, your children also have food phases. Giving healthy choices with food on the table, cutting out unhealthy snacks, and making meals more fun than a prison camp will teach your kid that food is lovely, pleasant.

Parents in Denmark sometimes say, to motivate children to eat, "You have to eat this food so that you are big and strong! You want to be big and powerful? "The parent tells the kid to flex her knees to show how strong she is and promises her that it comes from her greens and healthy foods. It works more frequently than you think!

Explain the Rules and Demand for Awareness

"Put your seat belt on." "No, I don't want that. "No." "Because you can be very hurt and have to go to the hospital if we have an accident. Want to go to the hospital? "No." (Put the seat belt firmly on.) The more you explain things, the better you can understand. This approach gives respect and helps you and your children to share a common goal (in this case, take a ride).

Getting Started

1. Make a plan of action.

What are your ideas for your kids? Include your partner and your own.

2. Are you hitting or hitting?

Hold a vow to stop. It is not appropriate and does not encourage faith and appreciation.

3. You shout too much?

Start vowing. Stop pledge. Only use it if appropriate. Yelling isn't good for anybody. Your kids are mirroring you; you are a model for them. If you want them to regulate and behave, you need to set the example of controlling yourself.

How can you stop screaming? Search for ways to reduce your own pain. Get more sleep. Get more sleep. Breathe. Breathe. Sleep more. Exercise more. Getaway some time. Getaway some time. Yelling and hitting are often the product of the absence of extra time to analyze and have the gap between the responses to help pick your answer.

If you feel close to bursting or shouting, take a deep breath. Go to another room and take a rest. If your friend will pass the baton, do it. Seek not to be in step with your punching and shouting values and always be firm on what you do or do not want your children to do. The partnership is important. It also helps because you can keep each other in check for your outbreaks more quickly. And if one of you is at the max and about to break, remind the other to take over peacefully. In a short time, you will begin to see your children behave more peacefully.

6.5 Tips for No Ultimatums

- Remember to differentiate the child's behavior. There's no bad child; there's only bad behavior. And there's bad parenting, too.
- Avoid power struggles. You won't find them if you don't look for power struggles. Win-win still say, not "How can I win? "Fourth. Don't blame the child for taking your own responsibility and next time trying to do better.
- Try to make sure children are inherently good Children should push limits and test rules. It's not terrible and deceptive. That's how they are rising.
- Learn to guide, nurture and educate your children. Don not just punish them and see them as more discipline is required. Try to find ways to handle complicated behavior. Do not call them "sneaky" or

"manipulative" or "terrible." The behavior is the actions; it is not the boy.

- Reframe Look for the best story about your kids and others. Learning how to reframe your children and showing them how to do so makes you more caring and healthier.
- Remember: the loop returns to you bad gets good. Poor begets poor. Worse begets worse. Power is out of power peace is quiet.
- Research shows that even one parent adopting the dominant style (not authoritarian) and maintaining her cool will make a big difference. Yet two are stronger yet!
- Write down all the ultimatums you use daily. Test the ultimatums. How are they identical to those used by your parents? How can you get them more positive?
- Consider always of your child's age. What can you expect of your child in relation to his or her age? Every era has a "style" of what is required of it. Kids aren't little people.
- Support all sorts of emotions Consider the feelings of your kid, whether or not she's in the mood you like. Everybody sometimes has a bad day, even babies. By not stressing it, you attract less attention to it and are more mindful of its self-regulation potential.
- Remember that opposition is a response to something Recall that protest is a way to communicate. It can also be a symbol of increased liberty. Instead of thinking of it as a horrible frustration, understand what it is.
- Put the wrong behavior into context has there been any changes in the life of your child that could lead to behavioral change?
- Know what snaps you It is important to know the causes. Where is your breaking point, and what can you do to get there? Do you need more food, relaxation or workout? Listen to your needs and ask for assistance.
- Say you are attentive, make sure you show your kid you are listening to her. For one, it's important to show her that she's heard and understood when she asks for something even though it can't. Say it, so she knows you heard it. You know. "I can tell that you want a lollipop, but I can imagine that. " Explain why something can't be done to your boy. Teach love, respect, and you will be valued more.

Chapter 7: Togetherness and Hygge

7.1 T Is for Togetherness and Hygge

As Maria first met the family of her husband and spent time with her in Denmark 13 years ago, the feeling was, to say the least, shocking. Hygge sig, or hygge, (pronounced "hooga"), meaning "to sleep together" was for them a way of life. She is cozying together involved lighting candles, playing games, enjoying nice food, having cake and tea and typically in a comfortable setting with each other. This large family would come together for days only to be warm without a great break. In the beginning, Maria thought this party odd, but after 13 years of studying the trend, we finally worked out the key for hygiene.

Maria's culture, being American, was very different. As a rule, they could only be around for a limited amount of time, after which they would need a break. They did so professionally, but they knew it was part of their way of life to take breaks and to do their own thing. Feeling the need to be together for a long time would almost have seemed a violation of their rights as Americans. This looked like a catastrophe formula and claims. He could not actually understand how the Danish families seemed to live together without further family drama for so long. Sure, someone had issues, problems or at least a neurotic propensity to talk over with friends and family around. There seemed to be very little negativity and no resentment, and they ran together like a well-oiled machine given how many people came together. What was going on in the world?

Could this pleasant time together be part of why the Danes have been the happiest people in the world so consistently voted on? The answer is a complete, yes!

Research shows that quality time with friends and family is one of the top predictors of well-being and satisfaction. This is not always necessary in our modern world, but the Danish Way blends sanitation into everyday life to ensure that.

7.2 Hyggge as a means of living

The word hygge dates back to the XIX century and originates from the Germanic word hyggja meaning "to remember or to feel satisfied." Hygge is something Danes understand in practice as well as in being it is part of their cultural base.

Since the Danes see hygiene as a way of life, they all try to make a comfortable time with family and friends. For starters, they work together at Christmas to ensure maximum relaxation. It's a team effort. It includes stuff like lighting the room with candles and good food, but it's also in their way. I try to help so that one or a few people do not feel like the only people who do the work. Older children are encouraged to play with the younger ones to support them. We try to play games everybody can enjoy, and everybody makes an effort to play even if they don't want to. The choice out of the game was not huge-light, it would not be "comfortable." They're trying to leave their personal issues behind and be constructive to stay away from too much conflict, and together they enjoy this cozy moment and want it to be. We can be concerned about our lives and stressors at days, and happiness comes from putting those moments aside and being with those we enjoy at the moment. To Danes, the ultimate goal is to have a warm and beautiful experience together, and this is a great example to our children.

Feeling connected to others gives our lives meaning and purpose, and that is why hygiene by Danes is so respected. The person is also respected, but without engagement and support from others, none of us as a whole can really be satisfied.

The notion of unity, if you think about it, is quite distinct from the individualistic ethos that constitutes a large part of the American culture.

The American Bedrock

The US was built on the ideology of self-confidence. If we are strong enough to succeed on our own, we do not really need others. Why should we focus on help if we can do it ourselves? They glorify individual achievement and self-fulfillment with words like "the self-made guy" and idolize an individual hero from politics and sport in all walks of life. If you listen to sports, the team effort rarely comes to you; it is the person who stands out, namely the famous quarterback or pitcher. It is the light that shines from the others. People who help to assist the celebrity frequently transform into flouted background noise. It is the hard work and survival of the fittest we most respect. Then we are born to aspire to be the light, to succeed. Geert Hofstede, a world-famous cultural scientist, concluded that the US has the highest level of individualism in the world in a very famous study on cultural differences. That's quite incredible. We are so conditioned to talk about "I," we probably don't even know.

This does not mean that the US has no unbelievably, strong community spirit. This simply points out that we are more programmed to think individualistically in cultural terms. For example, it's much more common, during a family reunion, to talk about how I feel than how we feel. We talk about things like me time or how to meet my desires, or how it makes me feel rather than how it makes us feel.

It is also fair to say that most of us would like to be "winners." We want our kids to win or at least to be the best and to stand out. That's quite natural.

What would not want that?

Who would not?

Look for a number of creative reasons nowadays for the number of awards in schools. We aspire to gain praise for something, whether it was the hottest laugh, the sweetest grin or the best jump roper in the school. It has become the very foundation of our society.

Additionally, how many of us would actually find the "gang unity" trophy? How many of us would measure the success of our child not how well he played but how well others played or how well the children were playing together?

Where you replace "We" for "I," then "Illness" is "Wellness."

There are many consequences for the definition of cohabitation and sanitation, but it is ultimately for the good of everyone. It leaves the drama at the door and sacrifices your individual needs and desires to make a group meeting more enjoyable. This is a much more enjoyable experience for your children. Teen drama, negativity and divisiveness don't please them. Kids are very pleased to be warm and together! And if you learn to hygienic, you will also be able to pass it on to your children one day.

There are a famous heaven and hell fable that illustrates this concept well. In the hell is a long table with a beautiful champagne, food and candles party, but the atmosphere is freezing. The men around the table are frail and emaciated, and the air is overflowing with a cacophony of moaning and screaming. They have very long sticks rather than arms, which prevent them from getting food into their mouths. Seek it as you could, it's pointless. They are all starving, given the rich abundance of food.

There is much the same scenario in heaven. There is still a long table and the celebration and the candles, but there are ridiculous people around the table.

They sing, and they chew.

The environment is warm and vibrant, with cuisine, wine and business everyone enjoying. The irony is that they too have very long arms sticks. Yet they eat each other instead of trying to feed themselves. A shift of perspective substituting "us" with "me" or "I" has converted hell into paradise in this simple metaphor.

Across Denmark, from an early stage on, children work on projects across communities that enable them to learn to help others and partake in collaboration and team building.

Teamwork in Denmark

Children are taught to look for the strengths and weaknesses of others and see how they can help people move further than just on the surface. Danes are also promoting modesty of their star students so that they are compassionate and caring for others. It's not hyggeligt just to look for yourself. In reality, Danes are worldwide known for being quick and polite to deal with. That's because they're great team members. They help others to help themselves, and even when they are stars, they are humble. And who doesn't enjoy a humble start?

Social groups are also an important part of Danish culture. Such classes, known as "foreningsliv," are focused on a common passion or interest.

The target may be fiscal, financial, academic or cultural.

Their role can be to improve something in society, for example in a political association, or to express oneself in a manner that suits the social needs of the community, such as in the choir or bridge club.

Statistics show that 79% of business leaders in Denmark were participating before the age of thirty in partnerships. 94%, 92% and 88% of managers who have participated with organizations agree that these years of participation have gained and created a strong network for their social skills and behavioral competencies.

Ninety-nine per cent of the governors of Denmark agree that membership in these charitable organizations enhances the professional skills of young people.

The sense of cooperation and partnership is seen from the classroom, workplace and family life in all facets of Danish culture. Seeing the family as a team creates a deep sense of belonging. Eat together, clean up together, spend time with each other these are Danish families ' daily ways of fostering a feeling of well-being.

Singing and Hygge

An interesting way for Danes to establish hygge is their love of music. If there is a song-worthy gathering, they will most probably sing, from Christmas dinners and birthdays to baptisms and weddings.

The songs they sing are often written for a purpose that is circulated and sung in a common melody. These home-made texts are often hilarious, and everybody discovers the words together while singing. Songs they sing come from a national songbook entitled "Højskolesangbogen," which dates back to the royalty and aristocracy festivals of late Middle Ages, but was expanded over time and is now more popular than ever before.

Nick Stewart of the University of Oxford Brookes has studied choir singers and discovered that singing together not only makes people happy, and it also makes them feel that they are part of a cohesive community. The synchronicity of moving and singing creates a strong sense of connection. In fact, experiments have shown that groups of singers can indeed synchronize their heartbeats when singing. Together, the "good" hormone oxytocin is released, reducing stress and growing feelings of trust and bonding. One only needs to try singing (once you're stupid), to feel such powerful effects.

Social Ties and Stress Levels

The level of happiness of the Danes is not the only evidence of the efficiency of unity and hygiene. A lot of research confirms this. Scientists at Brigham Young University and North Carolina University at Chapel Hill gathered data from 148 health outcomes experiments and their association with social relations. Together with more than 300,000 men and women across the developed world, these studies have shown that on average 50% more people with poor social links die earlier (approximately 7.5 years) than people with strong social ties. The lifespan gap is nearly as high as the mortality disparity between smokers and non-smokers. And the health risks associated with many other popular lifestyle factors such as lack of exercise, so obesity is greater than any.

Sheldon Cohen of Carnegie Mellon University subjected hundreds of healthy volunteers to the common cold virus, who had completed questionnaires describing their social lives and then quarantined them for several days, in another famous experiment in health and social relations. The findings have shown that the quarantined subjects with more social connections are less likely than those in their life to catch a cold.

The immune systems of people with many friends worked simply better. We could fight the cold virus better, often without symptoms. As stress hormones appear to influence the immune response, it is logical that a strong social life helps the immune system to remain strong physiological stress is monitored.

This influence was observed and validated by a research group in Chicago. Actually, social support helps to manage stress.

When we know that we have friends with whom we can speak or turn on support in difficult times, we are more willing to face challenges in life without breaking down. We're more durable. Feeling open to someone helps to lighten the burden we have. Most people strive to be stoic and to keep things close, but research shows that those who seek to be tough in a crisis suffer a great deal more than those who share feelings and are vulnerable to others.

New Moms and the Danish Way of Togetherness

In particular, the relaxing influence of the unification is noticeable in new mothers, who have unimaginable tension in line with their new role. There can be an overwhelming lack of sleep and all tasks in front of new parents. However, research shows that new mothers often react to this difficult period by reducing rather than increasing the amount of social support. This is paradoxical because it further aggravates the case. Support from friends, family members and parent groups was clearly demonstrated to help new mothers manage stress and thus to help them to see their children in a more positive light. This improves the quality of life of everyone, especially the growing child. The more parents get social support, and the healthier and happier the baby can develop.

When a woman gives birth in Denmark, a local sister gets her information and visits her for the first week to check in and see if she and the baby are safe.

More importantly, the midwife also gives her the names and contact data of all the women who have just had babies in her neighborhood, with information as to if she is the first, second, or third baby to make the women matched.

Such women form groups which meet once a week to discuss and support their experiences.

The other moms in the school are also supporters and test a mother if she doesn't.

They can call her or go home and ensure that she's all right and has contact with others with whom she can communicate. They are an important comfort in a very difficult time and an essential part of being a new mother in Denmark that makes all mothers and babies feel happy and safe.

7.3 The Danish Way of Hygge

We spoke a lot about social support, cohabitation and the value of hygge. But here is Maria's personal example because she knew what it is. It was a bright, fresh day. Maria lying under her husband's big plum tree in her baby sister's backyard, her young son and daughter were tucked between them. We were wrapped up like a swinging burrito, some with open eyes, and others with close doors. Maria put one foot out of the hammock lazily to hold them back and forth. The wind rocked the trees loudly; flickering rays of the sun shined in kaleidoscopic patterns on their faces through the leaves. It was a blend of touch, warm sounds and the smell of the downy hair of her baby son. The warmth of her husband's leg beside hers could feel her heartbeat. She held her daughter's foot, who was cuddled quietly with him. All of them were present.

"Oh, I see here you love some family hygge," she said as she came to welcome them for lunch. And that, Maria, felt it was hygge in a nutshell after thirteen years with her boyfriend.

It's both a feeling and a way of being. It eliminates all else's confusion and hysteria. He chooses to enjoy and respect the most important, meaningful moments of our lives those with our children and family and friends.

This keeps things easy, makes the mood optimistic and leaves our problems behind. It needs to be there at those moments, wants to be there and help to have a pleasant time.

With a large family, it takes effort, because, like all team projects, it works together to achieve a common goal. This is the opposite of being a person who stands out from the crowd. It must all be wanted and respected by everyone. Everyone has a part to play. It strengthens families significantly when we are all ready to contribute to having a comfortable moment together, which in turn affects our well-being and enjoyment drastically.

7.4 Tips for togetherness and hygge

- At the next meeting, make a pact with the whole team, not to "I," but to be at the moment to try to make things run smoothly and without argument. At the conclusion of this chapter, you can find the Hygge Oath or print it from thedanishway.com.
- All should agree to leave their everyday stressors at the door at this moment. Don't dwell on the bad things in your life or somebody else. Try not to dwell on problems or think too much about something. Everybody needs to make an effort to be together at that moment. Hold it bright, happy and accusative. Children embody this conduct and they feel safe and respected.
- Practice "pre-framing" Plan yourself and family for a meeting, so that you can make the most of it without throwing on your regular worldwide or personal drug glasses. Try to imagine what kind of interaction you will have and either consider or explore coping strategies, which will allow you to stay calm while you are there. Recall the stress-free family get-togethers greatly improve well-being. We are often trapped with different family members in our lives. Adjust it. Change it. Using empathy, reframing and preconception to help.
- Fun together when the entire family spends time together, play indoor and outdoor games in which everyone can participate. Set aside your personal preferences and just get out and play.
- Consider the room comfortable, with soft lighting, home-made decorations and décor, and food and drinks that you have cooked together.
- Just take a break anytime you feel the urge to lament, then, see where you can help. Alone, if everyone agrees, the level of happiness that you share as a family will make a big difference.

- Reframing is a truly powerful method if you get frustrated reframing. All can be reframed. Was the apple pie soggy? Everyone can use a spoon now! Has the football game rained out? Space for a Monopoly Fun Game! Recall that you pass it on to your children, allowing them to deal with their own emotional reactions.
- We also have so many toys (for adults and children), which drown simple things, as the wind sounds in the trees and the funny, sweet things our children do every day. Distractions take away the grooming, which deals with the most important and true issues. Keep it simple. Keep it simple.
- Stay current and inspire the children to remain present and useless games, DVDs, iPhones and iPads. These should be stopped in workshops so that the children can also be more involved. Play instead of games.
- Stay linked Seek to learn and practice together for a good time. Talking about sanitation together, the children can carry it on to better family interaction.
- Encourage play to Invite older children to play "in real life" with younger children, not on an electronic device. Give them pictures or allow them to play outside just make sure family playtime is free of technology or limited to certain times.
- Inspire team bonding. Organize more team building events to inspire children to work together. Build searches for scavengers, build a fort, and plan a tournament. Be imaginative. Be innovative.
- Confide and share when you're down or bad, rely on and share with your good friends and loved ones you trust. Note, this reduces stress and allows you to overcome it more easily. When the rough patch is over, share the story of how others helped you through with your kids.
- Start a mother community. Check your neighborhood for fellow moms and build a support network. This type of support has proven extremely beneficial, helping mothers face daily challenges and even see their children better.
- Teach your children that the family is a squad Instead of "everybody for themselves," allow all to join the family team, and teach your kids what role they can perform-how they can contribute and engage in various projects and events. This spirit of cooperation and co-operation makes everyone feel healthier and happier.
- . Celebrate everyday coexistence. Remember that hygge is not restricted to large family gatherings. It can be achieved with only one

or two people. Of example, one weekday you might announce a "hygge night." The concepts mentioned in this chapter are applied.

Where Do We Go from Here?

And so, again, the question arises. What has kept the Danes so long in the top of the satisfaction list after 40 years of being chosen as the happiest people in the world? As we saw in The Danish Way of Parenting, it's quite simply how their children are raised. It's a tradition that persists over the decades leading to self-confident, trustworthy, concentrated, content and resilient people and it can work for anyone.

It is important as parents to first look at our default settings, our natural inclinations as parents, so that we can see better where change is needed.

Having time to look inside the mirror and see what we replicate from our own family patterns is the first step to successful parental reform.

Once we have identified our default settings, PARENT principles provide simple, effective instruments to increase the happiness of our children and of ourselves.

Play helps children to develop many vital skills in life. Resilience, expertise in communicating and dealing and self-control are only few of the valuable lessons gained in unstructured play as well as stress management, which decreases children's chances of battling fear as adults.

Practice helps to develop an internal control locus, giving children trust in their own capabilities that lay the foundation for happiness.

Authenticity helps children to build a strong internal compass by learning to trust their feelings. To teach ourselves and our children honesty promotes a strong value of character. And remember all emotions are all right. In addition, different kinds of praise affect children differently in the way they are seen worldwide. Giving empty praise or focusing too much on smartness can make children feel unsafe and risky. Through celebrating systems, we encourage a more stable, more optimistic and robust person rather than a set one.

Reframing is a powerful way to change the perceptions of our children and our lives. How we choose to look at things influences what we act. Realist optimists ignore bad news, but simply focus on the other facts they have at hand and write a better, more caring tale about themselves, their children and life in general. Reframing will improve our social experience and make our lives and the lives of our children happy in the process. Moving on to the ability to reframe our children can be one of the best gifts we can give, fostering their future happiness and future generations.

Empathy is a central and primarily human instinct. While empathy has fallen in our society and the level of narcissism has increased, research has demonstrated that we are more connected to empathy than to egoism. They can better understand the insecurity in ourselves and in others by being less judgmental and less judging, which brings us closer together, build healthier, compassionate relationships and makes us all happier. Empathy teaches children to respect others and themselves, which gives a deeper sense of well-being.

Some ultimatums remember the fights for dominance will cause us to lose our patience. Most adults yell or use disciplinary physical punishment. We lose control, but we do not expect our kids. Trust and closeness towards their children are replaced with apprehension in an oppressive parenting style. This works short-term, but can have long-term consequences. The Danish more relaxed form of parenthood encourages child trust and endurance. Children who are respected and understood, who are supported in turn to understand and follow rules, develop a much stronger sense of self-control and eventually become happier, more emotionally stable adults.

Togetherness and Hygge are ways to encourage our closest connections, which are one of a person's greatest predictors of happiness. Through learning how to clean or relax, we will develop our family to make our children fun and unforgettable experiences. When we leave the "I" at the door and focus on the "us," we will remove a great deal of the unnecessary drama and animosity related to families. Happy families and strong social support provide happier children.

As we said before, maybe you already know or may not have heard of some of the concepts in this book.

You may already practice or practice some of the Danish methods. We are confident that you are on a right track to raise happy babies, if you take even some of the approaches from this book and integrate them into your life.

To order to raise healthier, healthier babies, we believe that parents and teachers should help each other together. Support is needed for all of us. In building a community in order to practice these values, we will create some of the happiest people in our own backyards in the world. We hope you're going to get on board and help us to achieve it!

Hygge Oath

Hygge is the special Danish expression for a particular type of harmony. Picture hygge being a place the family will visit. The special room will be more hygienic if everybody knows and tries to conform to the hygiene laws. The hygiene can be discussed and thought about in advance, so everyone who enters the hygiene space for a family dinner, weekend barbeque, or simple family reunion will understand the "ground rules." If everyone knows that hygiene is time, everyone can work to foster proximity for the sake of the whole family. The foregoing is an example of a hygiene vow for the household. Adapt it to your own household and let the harmony continue.

We agree to hygge "Sunday dinner." As a team, we promise to help each other build a comfortable environment in which everyone feels safe, and nobody has to look out for them.

- We agree to try to do so.
- Turn mobile and iPads off.
- Leave us at the door to our drama. Some days we dwell on our issues. Hygge aims to create a safe place for relaxing and leaving stressful things outside.
- Don't complain unnecessarily.
- Seek ways to help so that nobody gets stuck to do all the job.
- If we're inside, light candles.
- Try to enjoy food and drink intentionally.
- Don't lift controversial issues such as elections. Everything that creates a struggle or an argument is not hygienic. At other moments, we can have these conversations.
- Say and say funny, wonderful and uplifting stories from the past.
- Don't praise too much. Subtly divisive praising can be.
- Not rivalry (think "us" not "me"). Not competition.
- Don't talk badly or dwell on negative.
- Play games that can be enjoyed by the whole community.
- Make a conscious effort to express gratitude to the people around us who love us.

8.Conclusion

Therefore, the question arises again. Despite 40 years of voting as the happiest people in the world, what has stopped the Danes in the top positions for so long? As I saw in The Danish way of parenting, it's the way they raise their children very clearly. It is a legacy that continues over the generations, which leads to self-confident, confident, centered, happy and resilient adults and that can work for anyone.

It is important, as parents that we first examine our default conditions, our natural inclinations as parents so that we can better see where changes are needed. The first step towards positive change and a happy childhood are taking the time to look in the mirror and see what we mimic from our own family experiences.

Once our default settings have been established, PARENT values offer simple and effective mechanisms for promoting joy in our children and ourselves.

As I stated earlier, you might already know or have not yet heard of some of the topics in this book. I am confident that you will be on the right track to raise happy kids if you take some of the methodologies from this book and integrate them into your life. I believe parents and teachers will work together to promote the Danish Way to bring up happier and more resilient children. Support is needed for all of us. In building a community in order to practice these values, we will create some of the happiest people in our own backyards in the world. I hope you are going to get on board and help us do it!

The Danish Way of Parenting provides a fantastic solution to contemporary parenting, which is a book that contributes to the true origins of family harmony.

Everybody around the globe will learn from the precious wisdom found in this book. Concepts like reframing and grooming are beneficial for communities of all backgrounds. It is great that Danish parenthood shares so much with Good Parenthood! This book I highly recommend! "The Danish Circulation allows parents worldwide to test their own preferences and take the entire infant into consideration.

An appreciation of the value of free playing is a breath of fresh air at a time of intense and overwhelming young children. I thought this book was a clear, very useful and intelligent guide on how to improve your own level of happiness as a parent, and how to encourage happier children in Danish. I would like to recommend this book to anyone who wants the best prospects of a happy life for themselves and/or their children.

9.References

- O'Keeffe, A. (n.d.). *The Danish Way of Parenting review – how to raise the world's happiest kids.* [online] the Guardian. Available at: https://www.theguardian.com/books/2016/aug/06/danish-way-of-parenting-review.

- HARDING, N. (n.d.). *UK couple change family routine as they adopt The Danish Way of Parenting.* [online] The Sun. Available at: https://www.thesun.co.uk/living/1501594/uk-couple-change-family-routine-as-they-adopt-the-danish-way-of-parenting/.

- HealthyWay. (n.d.). *Want To Raise Happier Kids? Parent Like The Danish.* [online] Available at: https://www.healthyway.com/content/want-to-raise-happier-kids-parent-like-the-danish/.

- Sandra M. Bell - Hypnotherapist. (n.d.). *Raise Happy Kids, The Danish Way | Sandra M. Bell - Hypnotherapist.* [online] Available at: **https://www.sandrambell.com/raise-happy-kids-the-danish-way/.**

- Psychology Today. (n.d.). *Can Parenting the Danish Way Be Applied Elsewhere?.* [online] Available at: **https://www.psychologytoday.com/us/blog/neuro-behavioral-betterment/201705/can-parenting-the-danish-way-be-applied-elsewhere.**

10: References

The Brain before Birth: Using fMRI to Explore the Secrets of Fetal Neurodevelopment. from **https://ehp.niehs.nih.gov/doi/10.1289/EHP2268**

Fetal Brain Development - Nervous System. Retrieved from **https://www.whattoexpect.com/pregnancy/fetal-development/fetal-brain-nervous-system/**

5 Stages of Human Brain Development. Retrieved, from **https://nancyguberti.com/5-stages-of-human-brain-development/**

Cold, F., Health, E., Disease, H., Disease, L., Management, P., & Conditions, S. et al. Cynicism Starts Early in Children. Retrieved from **https://www.webmd.com/parenting/news/20050527/cynicism-starts-early-in-children#1**

Child Has a Negative Attitude - Focus on the Family. Retrieved from **https://www.focusonthefamily.com/family-qa/child-has-a-negative-attitude/**

Retrieved from **https://www.who.int/maternal_child_adolescent/child/nurturing-care-framework-first-draft.pdf**

CPSIA information can be obtained
at www.ICGtesting.com
Printed in the USA
LVHW050007231220
674915LV00032B/1031